ESCAPE

from *Grief*

Prison

A Story of Love, Loss, and Healing

To Terry,
Life goes on!
Gail Norwood

GAIL NORWOOD

ISBN 978-1-63814-621-6 (Paperback)
ISBN 978-1-63814-623-0 (Hardcover)
ISBN 978-1-63814-622-3 (Digital)

Covenant Books
11661 Hwy 707
Murrells Inlet, SC 29576
www.covenantbooks.com

CONTENTS

ACKNOWLEDGMENTS

$\mathcal{N}$ow I can say I have given birth three times; I had two girls and a book!

When I first considered the possibility of writing down all my feelings and ideas into a cohesive form, I had no idea how many people would ultimately contribute to its completion. The various gifts of discernment, insight, and attention to detail from my support team has made me grateful beyond measure.

After months of outlines, early notes, and feeling overwhelmed, I realized I needed help, and I welcomed the assistance of my book coach. Michelle Vandepas, thank you for your steadfast guidance and inspiration.

With a fresh approach, Editor Laurie Knight skillfully offered structural and developmental suggestions along with fine-tuning that helped the words take form. Many thanks, Laurie.

When I needed feedback on early drafts, I could count on so many of my close friends and family who gave their time and talent to urge me along. You know who you are, and I appreciate your input and enthusiasm more than you will ever know.

To Sandra Jarvis and the professional staff at Covenant Books, Inc., I offer my deepest gratitude for your valuable role in bringing my manuscript successfully through the many stages of book production.

And mostly, to my daughters, Mary Evelyn and Amy, I am so grateful to you for initially helping me think through the possibilities and the challenges inherent in this endeavor and bolstering my confidence as I inched forward toward them both. And when I told you I hoped you'd be proud of me one day for this prodigious effort, you let me know you were proud of me for even trying.

THE BEGINNING

Serendipity led me to
the True Story Café.
Intrigued by the name,
I inched closer.
A sign in the window
announced
"Today's Special"
but I was too far away
to read the words.
I paused, then turned
toward home.
As I walked, it followed me.
It troubled me.
It was all I could
think about.
What is the true story?

I don't want to talk about grief. Grief is
dark and sad and lonely. It is the last thing I

want to talk about. Something more cheerful like bluebirds and snowflakes are more to my liking. But at this season of my life, it is the tight grip of grief and loss that holds me hostage and begs me to speak of it. Dealing with great loss of any kind is a part of our humanity that most of us cannot avoid. Perhaps this experience has already befallen you, or it may be yet to come. Either way, we are assured it is an authentic component of our earthly existence. With no one-size-fits-all remedy available, we are presented with a multitude of coping strategies. It is up to us to find the path to healing that feels right and works best for us. For me, it included writing this book.

For years, I imagined my passion for gardening would provide ample material for any initial attempt I might take at writing a book. I had always heard one should write about what one knows. Even though I knew a lot about gardening, inspiration eluded me, and the idea withered. Then unexpectedly, life took a turn, and now what I know a lot about is managing and surviving grief. In fact, when the idea to write this book first began to germinate within me, I solidly objected. I had serious doubts. Could I create a book on a topic so forlorn, so dire? My upbeat personality was not buying it. But life had brought me here, and there was no making it go away. I felt compelled to tell my story and hoped it might in some way soothe the suffering souls of my brothers and sisters caught in the same shackles. In the timeless classic *Peter Pan*, author J. M. Barrie says, "All the world is made of faith, and trust, and pixie dust." Much like enchanted pixie dust infused with a healthy dose of faith and trust, I will sprinkle out my message of positive healing from loss in hopes that it will fall gently upon those who mourn. Like Wendy, John, and Michael, let them be lifted up and learn to fly again. "Second star to the right and straight on 'til morning."

Within these pages, some nontraditional references may be found that invite the opportunity to pause and think in a different way. My path to the depths of my soul was a great awakening. I was shaken to my core. Then forced self-awareness prompted me to shine a light on my role in my own healing. What was I doing to help or hinder? What more could I do to foster my healthy recovery? A startling realization settled in as I learned that most of us only reach the tip of the iceberg in our efforts to allow and promote our own physical, emotional, and spiritual growth. Too often we choose a pill or a quick fix in lieu of "doing the work." There is so much we can gain when we let go of deep-rooted, limiting thoughts and open our hearts and minds to the abundant resources available.

Charlie Brown was right on with his signature exclamation, "Good Grief!" This oxymoron demonstrates the paradox that grief is usually not thought of as good. But this self-contradictory statement may prove true. With no special training in grief therapy, I do not claim to be an expert, but I am a recent graduate of the School of Hard Knocks. I have been steeped in grief, and I know whereof I speak. I have known bad grief and good grief. Rescued by the *good grief* I have discovered and from a place of genuine hope, I bring forth my story.

Can there be such a thing as *good grief?* I identified with the phrase and the concept of adopting a positive posture for transcend-

ing grief, undeniably one of life's most difficult challenges. We know grief to be a normal
time in our lives spent coping with a serious
loss. A very serious loss. Usually, a life-changing loss. Not limited to the anguish of losing
a loved one, it often involves a job, divorce, a
close relationship, one's health, or other fates.
We are suddenly relegated against our will to
this unfamiliar territory, and there is really
nothing *good* about it. Or is there?

Bereavement is a necessary time for us
to pause, feel our feelings, and endure challenging emotions in order to get to the other
side of the pain and sadness. But is there any
goodness in it, and can we make an effort
to reach out and grab that goodness? Can
we focus on the healing power of this sacred
time and resist the inclination to lean into the
suffering that often follows? Can we shift our
awareness of grief to include the discovery
that we have choices in this most life-changing journey, and that these choices can make
all the difference in how we endure?

I found myself following society's unspo-
ken *grief code of conduct*, surrendering to the
subtle suggestion that I was expected to do so

to properly honor my husband's memory and our abiding marriage. I did not know I had a choice. I did not know there were things I could do to nurture myself to a place of gentle healing. I totally accepted the concept that grief is most likely going to unfold in a certain predictable way, and I better just fasten my seat belt and hold on tight. It is all there in the *Grief Prison Handbook*. I started to feel the walls close in around me but at first did not recognize what was happening and did nothing about it.

After years in emotional confinement, I discovered that even though we cannot wish grief away, if we are able and willing to seek out and practice healthy coping mechanisms, we will find that tools are indeed there to help us minimize the emotional and even physical damage that can occur. Then we can, from this higher place of healing, discover and internalize the truths revealed to us. The keys of *good grief* can unlock that internal prison door and allow us to escape. Escape from excessive or complicated grieving. Escape from the confines of outdated social mores that confuse and restrict us. Escape from unnecessary self-imposed expectations. Escape from the influence of words that do not speak our truth. Escape from debilitating solitary confinement. And most of all, escape from the fear of letting go of our loss and opening the way to a new life.

1

Welcome to the Dark Side

If Only You Knew the
Power of the Dark Side.

—Darth Vader,
Star Wars Episode V: The
Empire Strikes Back

These ominous words portend a foreboding presence. Power and darkness come together to create a daunting force. It is a force I wish I had never known. It is a force that robbed me of my very spirit. It is a force that dominated my life for months—and years—that followed my husband's death. Over three years would pass before I would even begin to feel a desire to live again. Until then, I found the thundering aloneness disarming. The realization that Mike and I would not be living out our lives together as planned left me traumatized. I did not know how to stop saying "we" or "us," and each time I uttered those words, it was a jolting reminder of the fact that there was no longer a "we" or an "us." I would soon discover the power of the *dark side*. I would soon discover the *dark side of grief*.

The crying was incessant. Would it be a one-tissue-box day or a two-tissue-box day? My eyelashes gradually fell away during the washout. I laid in bed at night sleepless and sobbing and looked up to the heavens to admonish him with "Look what you have done to me! How could you leave me here alone?" This was so *not* me, and yet sadly now, it was. Shock and disbelief degenerated into depression. I had never been so low.

As insult to injury, I fell victim to the unrelenting fatigue and weariness that can befall a new widow or widower or anyone suffering a great loss. Often sleep would not come, forcing long restless hours, unable to stave off the memories. Or conversely, sleep fell so hard and long that days melted into a string of black pearly abandon. It became impossible to distinguish the blur between mental and physical exhaustion. The never-ending enervation resonates in this lullaby I used to sing to my babies...

> Bed is too small for
> my tiredness, give me
> a hilltop with trees.
> Tuck a cloud up under
> my chin—Lord, blow
> the moon out please.
>
> Rock me to sleep in a
> cradle of dreams, sing
> me a lullaby of leaves,
> Tuck a cloud up under
> my chin—Lord, blow
> the moon out please.
> (Author Unknown)

Oh Lord, hear me! Please blow the moon out, bury me in a dreamless sleep, and just make it all go away. That is my prayer. Amen.

We lost him in the depth of November—a cold, weary November. Then with a slow Scrooge-like tempo, the holiday season dragged by. For the month of December, I moved in with my daughter Amy and her family who lived nearby. Every few days, I went home for a few hours to check the mail and have some alone time. Our beautiful home, once the scene of festive family holidays with all the joy and trimmings of this magical season now sat cold, empty, and forsaken, a painful a reminder of happier times. I looked out the window, and even the garden appeared forlorn with sadness and seemed to cry out a solemn lament of its own. No one ventured outside as in past years to cut boughs off our brilliant American holly bush or trim blue cedar berries and foliage for table arrangements. There were no red nandinas, painted gold then displayed on the mantle over the fireplace above the stockings. This year, there was no bringing the garden inside to add the special touches only Mother Nature can provide. This formerly well-loved home and garden reeked of abandonment, and oh, how I could relate. But fortunately, I could leave this behind at least for now as I pulled into Amy and Don's driveway. Cheerfully decorated for the holidays, their home was my haven. A tall twinkling tree was surrounded by flickering candles, colorful ribbons on bright gifts, and a comforting warmth emanating from the fireplace. The ten-month-old baby and his three-year-old brother were my delight. There I could just be in the moment and try to forget the haunting events of recent weeks.

I was not ready to go back to that tomb of a home yet, so in early January, I drove to Georgia where my older daughter lived. Time with Mary Evelyn's family for a couple of weeks was just what I needed. Being with both our daughters and their families provided a powerful antidote. But driving back and forth alone was hard, and I hoped the radio would keep me from thinking and crying. Song after song spoke of love. I could not listen! Lyrics dripped with emotions about wanting someone, loving someone, or missing someone. The six-hour drive to Georgia loomed heavy with a daunting dread. I turned to audio books and indulged in the distraction. One after the other, they filled the hours with stories and characters transporting me to another place, a place where I would not be alone with my thoughts. I sought respite from the fateful *dark side*, which was following me like an inexorable shadow.

It felt so good to be with Mary Evelyn and Andy's family in their beautiful home with our two older grandkids, six and eight. Our grandson mournfully repeated with his head lowered, "I miss Papa," and our only granddaughter sweetly comforted me, clasping her small soft hand in mine. They spoiled me with consoling creature comforts and loving together time. My girls were suffering their own grief at suddenly losing their father but coping differently, as they juggled their maternal duties with unfamiliar waves of shock and sadness. It cut like a knife when we all realized that Mike was the only grandfather remaining in the two families, and now there would no longer be any grandfather for our four grandchildren in their young or future lives.

I went to Georgia armed with Mike's files and records. The task of preparing his taxes, closing his accounts and estate only added to my emotional trauma. It forced me to state again and again to some stranger on the phone that he has died and endure their canned condolences. I broke down every time, handing the phone to my daughter, unable to continue. Confusing and endless paperwork along with awkward phone calls were only tolerated and accomplished thanks to Mary Evelyn's attentive care.

Unable to delay any longer, I reluctantly returned to Chapel Hill later that month. This would undoubtedly be the hardest step, returning there alone to face my new reality. I could not tell if our clocks were ticking as before, but I knew the hours seemed oddly long and still as the weeks flew by. Being suspended in this warped dimension of time was unlike anything I had ever known.

A *bleak midwinter* silently advanced and settled in, both seasonally and in my soul. Gray, dreary January days reflected my dismal mood. Like a tomb, it was cold in the house and cold in my soul. Even the garden seemed to whimper softly as I slipped back to say hello upon my return. Dark and dormant as it had ever been, I sensed a palpable dirge in the wintry woodland, descending like a cold soft rain. Retreating inside through the well-worn back door, I was struck at the sudden realization that I was the sole inhabitant of our family home. It was almost too much to bear. Somber words by English poet Christina Rossetti (1872) filled my mind.

> In the bleak mid-winter
> Frosty wind made moan.
> Earth stood hard as iron
> Water like a stone.
> Snow had fallen,
> snow on snow,
> Snow on snow,
> In the bleak mid-winter
> Long ago.

My heart as hard as iron, my teardrops like a stone. Grief had fallen, grief on grief, in my personal bleak midwinter. So cold, so hard, so bleak.

The sobering reality of his death consumed me. Losing the presence of this man I had loved my whole adult life was bad enough, but soon I discovered other casualties. I was suddenly in a holding cell—single, no longer part of a couple as I had been since age twenty-one. It felt odd to be single again, a reaction that surprised me. The Social Security paperwork informed me, "Your marriage was terminated Nov. 23, 2013." I reeled at those words, which fell upon me like a forceful gavel slamming down hard with some cruel final verdict. *Till death do us part... Our marriage wasn't* over, I thought, *he was just gone.* In my heart, we were still married. I kept *Mrs.* in my name and proudly wore my wedding ring. Not only had our current life together expired, but any future life together had perished as well. This imposed solitary living situation was unpleasant, unexpected, and unwelcome. His untimely passing robbed us of any cherished plans and dreams for our later years. One by one, they withered and blew away with that cold November wind. Our herb garden sundial falsely proclaimed, "Grow old along with me, the best is yet to be."

I became a shut in. I did not want to see or talk to anyone except my family and my closest friends. The phone would ring but went unanswered. If a message was left, I would listen later, when I could cry quietly to myself. A follow-up e-mail to the caller conveyed my thanks and my unreadiness to talk. The persistent nagging phone was ignored until people quit calling. Neighbors stopped by, but I resisted answering the door. Sometimes I cracked it open, only to reveal my tear-stained face and offer my apologies. I dropped out of all meetings and activities—no church, no workouts at the gym, no lunches with friends. Generous invitations finally stopped coming as I turned down one after the other. My emotions were out of control, and I found solace in my own solitary lockdown.

Months passed, and I eventually opened up to an occasional visit from a close friend or two. The kitchen table was set with a fresh box of tissues next to the pot of tea and stack of grief books. To share with them "how I was doing" was impossible without a predictable breakdown. Did they *truly* want to know anyway? I told them I was fine, even if I wasn't. I am not sure I knew what *fine* was anymore. But I did know they could not fix it for me. No one could. This was my dark trek, and I had to find my own way. As months passed, my circle slowly widened. Supportive and comforting, I welcomed their love and friendship appreciating that they wanted to do more. I tried to explain that their being there was all I wanted, and everything I needed. The rest was up to me.

During these visits, I received a surprising and unwelcome prediction, which more than one person delivered, containing this warning: *The third year is the worst.* Stunned at the very thought of it, my initial reaction was that it would be impossible for anything to be worse than this first year. Was this supposed to comfort me? Why would people say this? The dismal forecast was oppressive, but I did not challenge it in my weak and gullible state. This living *hell* is going to persist for at least three years and become even worse? Unconscionable. The faceless *judge* presiding over the *court of conventional wisdom* had just sentenced me to a mandatory three years in *grief prison* with no chance of parole even with good behavior. With defiant submission, I tipped my hat to the power of suggestion—you have won again. Any truth about the integrity of our individual grief journeys was hereby challenged. To suggest such a general timeline at all refutes the notion that we are traveling this road by our own clock. Such damnation to the dreaded *purgatory* hastened my swirling downward spin.

Well-meaning friends gave me their favorite books on grief. The stack grew and grew. One after the other explored this vast abyss of brokenheartedness that for most of us in life is unavoidable. Hopefully within them there was something to discover about how to best navigate this raw, desperate, emotional terrain. I began to comprehend the magnitude of bereavement in the human experience and realized I was not alone. It was clear I was fortunate to have made it this far in my life without a more serious loss than the natural passing of my parents in their advanced age. That was hard enough. At sixty-four years old, I gave thanks that until the present time, I had lived a satisfying, content life. Suddenly now, my name was high on the docket in the *court of broken hearts.*

A neighbor came by on a walk and saw me in the front yard. She asked how I was doing. We chatted then she inquired if I was going to sell the house. When I told her I had no plans to do so, she was visibly shocked and surprised. With a gasp, she blurted, "You're *not* going to stay in this big old empty house, all by yourself, are you?" with a big emphasis on *are you?* And there it was—the expectation from someone I did not even know very well, that just because I was single again, I should give up my house. I felt betrayed and blindsided by the implication that I should automatically downsize, just because I was now alone. This was my beloved home of over two decades and the homeplace for my two daughters and their families. The garden was my pride and joy and could not move with me. Holiday gatherings could still be held here, and they could all spend the night as they had always done. I did not want to give that up. My grandchildren still loved coming here as they had done since they were babies, chasing butterflies, enjoying ice cream bars in the tree house, riding double on the swing. A smaller place just would *not* be the same and should not be imposed upon me or my family. As long as I could manage physically and financially to stay in my dream house and garden, it was my choice, and I would do so.

I opted not to attend support meetings. My reading and contemplations coupled with my family and inner circle of friends provided generous support, which I considered sufficient. I abhorred falling apart in front of people I did not know, or did not know well, no matter the circumstances. Clearly, my crying was not under control, and to openly expose my feelings felt vulnerable. My isolation took a stronghold. My world grew darker and darker. The G-monster was becoming a formidable foe. Know thine enemy? I did not...

Our beautiful garden on two acres was shamefully neglected. I drew solace from being in the garden and wandered back there often, but I lacked the motivation or energy to keep up the routine chores. I was too depressed to even realize how much I was letting it go. My energy level was tanked, I often did not feel well, and I just could not rally. The bare minimum was done, and I was grateful to discover that Mother Nature can be graciously forgiving. Likewise, there was no welcoming wreath on the front door, and the footed urns nearby remained flowerless. Our American flag was not displayed for years, and decorative outdoor pillows lay dormant in the storage shed. The despondency eating away at me on the inside was showing up on the outside, for all to see.

Despondency also shows up in the wardrobe. Now I know why people wear black in mourning. I considered it a traditional or cultural statement until I experienced it myself. Now I understand there is more to it than just following a custom. When I was in the *dark side* after losing Mike, I did not care about what I wore each day, and what I did wear was strictly drab and functional. Typical prison garb. For me, the classic white and black stripes morphed into all black. All the bright, colorful tops and sweaters were stuffed to the back of my closet. Even seeing the colors offended me. The jewelry box remained shut and shoved aside. I wore only my wedding ring and a necklace Mike had given me. Like smiling, it just felt wrong. If I dressed for errands, I went in simple dark clothes and shunned wearing anything I would consider nice. It was my version of the

symbolic ancient sackcloth, a biblical reference to a rough, uncomfortable fabric worn
by those in mourning or repentance. I get it
now. Cheerful or stylish clothes represented
the opposite of my state of mind. Bleak and
dark on the inside, bleak and dark on the
outside.

My typical seasonal maintenance routine
was completely derailed. Without realizing
it until much later, I totally abandoned my
treasured practice of bluebird watching and
tending. For years, I had successfully attracted
these glorious creatures, cleaned and cared for
the five boxes, and provided mealworms and
homemade suet cakes to nourish them. Then
I watched with joy as the new babies hatched
and fledged. Strangely, I do not even remember thinking about my beloved pastime, or
even missing it, during my years in the *dark
side*. So far from that place of joy, I could not
even hear them sing. Gradually, the nesting
boxes reeked with uncleanliness and disrepair, and eventually, they were overtaken by

aggressive barn swallows. Years later, I realized with great regret what I had unintentionally allowed to happen.

My religious upbringing coupled with an innate desire to do the right thing influenced me greatly during this time. My straight and narrow nature was speaking up and telling me to be a *good girl*. But my strong moral compass betrayed me. It pointed the way, a way that seemed positive at first but turned out to a negative experience. Accordingly, I felt I should explore available coping mechanisms and follow the rules and guidelines. The Kübler-Ross stages of grief were well-known to me, but it had gotten personal. While it is widely proclaimed that we can each go through the stages at our own pace and in our own time, there often remains the subtle aftertaste, an inference not to stray too far from the prescribed steps. Similarly, while many grief books contain uplifting messages of encouragement, reading between the lines frequently reveals whispers of caution. Thinly veiled, well-chosen words advise the reader not to hurry through the journey or bypass any steps. To do so would only cause delay in healing or a resurgence of unresolved issues down the road.

But wait, I thought I could go at my own pace? That is how all the grief books begin, right? Or you may read that it is best not to shut out comforting friends because of your pride or any other reason, for to try to "go it alone" would be asking for a hard time. I was met with confusion at every turn. My introverted, broken self might prefer more alone time than these writers may deem "acceptable." Some not-so-subtle authors go so far as to exclaim a caveat similar to this: Proceed however you please and do what you think is right for you, but do not kid yourself, it will not be over soon, it will not be easy, and it will not be without great pain and consequence.

Message received, loud and clear.

The power of suggestion looms large in our fragile impressionable minds during bereavement. Regrettably, those words of warnings and implications set me on a destructive path. The already vulnerable and distraught me embraced these cautions and warnings wholeheartedly because it sounded like the "right" thing to do—tried and true. What did I know of this? Let's hear from the experts! If the grief books said with authority that this was not going to be easy or fast, I believed them. If the predetermined stages of grief were laid out before me as a road map, who was I to question the progression? If the pamphlets warned against moving through the process too fast, I took it to heart—I took it all to heart—and proceeded to follow the rules. I vowed to continue my grief journey with full force, not bypassing anything. I consciously played out each stage of grief with complete aplomb. I felt the feelings sagaciously, probably experiencing them more acutely than necessary. Tears flowed and flowed when perhaps some moderation was in order. I dedicated myself to reading all the right books and checked them off my list. I proclaimed that I would get an emotional PhD in grief and slam dunk this monster. If this is what is best for me, my healing and my desire to honor Mike's life and our marriage, then so be it.

Little did I know what a dark and dangerous road was ahead. Even more resolute to stay isolated and deal with this in the way I had grown comfortable, I limped forward. Determined to do the best job possible at the grief game, I sensed a queasy motivation. The bottom line is that I thought this was how I was *supposed* to react. But instead, I overreacted. A few expressions of my deep loss were paid for with an even greater withdrawal from my emotional bank account.

For instance, a memorial photo book I made for Mike's remembrance took far too much of a toll on me, in the difficult and lengthy process coupled with my efforts to make it perfect. Elaborate and numerous thank-you notes painstakingly composed and sent with our fortieth anniversary photo, a memorial prayer card and other inserts, left me completely spent. Phone calls to extended family who were worried about me reopened the wounds and were excruciating, emotional, and flooded with tears. I told several close friends, "See you in a year." I clearly did not want to see them any sooner. I was full throttle in grief mode. I was taking it so hard.

Too hard. I followed protocol instead of following my heart. I did not know that was an option. As I held on to the "should," I lost sight of my choice to do it my way. These tributes to Mike and our lives together were lovingly offered but came with a high price. It was all-consuming and profoundly exhausting. I sank deeper.

I took to staring out the window. Any window, every window. Just staring aimlessly at nothing. Not looking for anything, not finding anything. Like a magnet, I was drawn there, as if being called somehow to pause and rest. Then in a timeless daze, I lingered. I was trapped, but I could not recognize that *I* had trapped myself. There was a peaceful calm about it. Perhaps it was a benevolent subconscious break from raw memories that would not be suppressed or a break from real or imagined vicissitudes that may await me. It was part of feeling numb and stuck. I saw the squirrels chasing each other and the wind dancing in the trees. They brought my attention to my poor, untended garden full of fallen leaves and plant debris in every bed. The tidy borders and rock edges of the paths were hidden beneath, waiting to be loved again. But I just could not do it yet—I only kept staring as inertia swallowed me whole.

Memories, tears, and loss of direction conspired to define my new identity. I was spinning out of control, and everyday life was so tentative. It was one step forward and two steps back. Only much later did I hear about *traditional* or *normal* grief as opposed to *complicated* grief. Stuck in the middle of something so complex, one struggles to process the status quo. A complicated grief is one that may last beyond a year and be more severe than the more common normal grief. This condition is sometimes referred to as persistent complex bereavement disorder. Symptoms are long-lasting, and return to normalcy is delayed. In traditional grief, symptoms start to fade naturally and healing occurs. I did not know it at that time, but I was entering a period of complicated grief.

During the second year, I became aware that I was exhibiting some PTSD symptoms, not unusual in complicated grief. My memory was completely void of certain events and conversations from the previous year, something I learned only when my daughters informed me of such. I failed to pay some bills and never got the car inspected or registered resulting in my getting a ticket. I had no idea about my delinquent actions, not even able to remember receiving the bill or the registration notice. Year one was blurry at best. Year two was not much better. I was hobbling. My daughter had given me a holiday platter for Christmas, but the next season, I found it packed away and wondered where it came from or how I got it. I did not remember ever having seen it before. I thought perhaps I bought it after Christmas on sale and just stuck it in the closet but did not remember doing so. I wrapped it up and gave it to Amy. She took one look at it and said, "Oh, Mom, I gave this to *you* last year, don't you remember?" No, I did not.

Sometimes it takes an earthquake to jolt us awake, and for me, that moment came when the mammogram technician found just the tiniest suspicious area. A complicated biopsy followed, then the wait for results. I was home alone when the phone call came. Absolutely nothing can prepare you for that moment when you hear, "I'm sorry, it's malignant." Waves of distress and disbelief overtook me once again, tearing the floor from underneath me. Terrified of what might be ahead, I questioned my mortality. Surgery and radiation followed, but thankfully, I was spared chemo treatments. It was very small and caught early, so my prognosis was good. I began a five-year course of the chemo drug tamoxifen, which was well-known for negative side effects. In addition, I would have years of more frequent diagnostic mammograms, petrified with each one that they might find something. The entire scenario caused me significant anguish. The fear and anxiety I experienced during that medical nightmare was hard to bear on top of my sentence in bondage to grief. This was grief upon grief. Sheer layers of grief. I was already struggling and then this. My family was supportive and helpful, but it was not a substitute for having Mike beside me to help navigate this dire strait. I silently cursed him for leaving me to endure this all alone. I was facing a crisis, a cancer diagnosis with all its inherent fear and uncertainty. This earthquake had shaken my world, leaving internal rubble and aftershocks in its wake.

It is no secret that mental anguish, including grief, can have a negative effect on the body. We have all heard of "dying of a broken heart." No doctor ever told me that the breast cancer had been caused by my loss and the subsequent long months of emotional suffering, but I knew it was at least partly responsible. In fact, they would not acknowledge any connection. But no one and nothing can ever convince me otherwise. It is widely noted that many people who exhibit a sudden cancer or some other physical illness have endured some defined trauma in the prior year or two. A quick Google search reveals how damaging grief can be on our bodies, especially in the heart region. High blood pressure, increased stress hormones, along with joint and muscle pain, are just the beginning, eventually wearing down our immune systems allowing even more complications. In extreme cases "broken heart syndrome" may occur mimicking a heart attack.

Concurrently, I developed severe pain in one hip and soreness in the opposite knee. It started a few months after losing Mike, but over the next two years, it continued to worsen. I tried over-the-counter meds that helped somewhat, but the pain persisted. Finally, I saw an orthopedic doctor who prescribed physical therapy for several weeks, coupled with cortisone shots, which helped temporarily. The chronic pain continued to worsen. An MRI did not reveal a cause. Later that summer, they confirmed no diagnosis and said there was nothing else they could do for me. I was told to go home and come back for another cortisone shot in three months.

I had undergone so much cortisone treatment that my arms and hands were covered with dark red blotches where the tiniest contact with anything caused an abrasion. Even my purse handle accidentally touching my forearm left a mark for weeks. This, combined with the unrelenting pain, prompted a solid desperation. I felt lost and out of options. My mobility was extremely compromised. It was difficult to get around the house, especially going up the stairs to do laundry or work at my computer. Unable to do anything in the garden, I watched it fall deeper into neglect and overgrowth. In disbelief, I actually entertained the thought of getting a walker. The truth was, I could not walk. Every step was debilitating pain. Even an old set of crutches did not help as neither leg was strong. To get around the house during the day, I held on to and put my weight on a counter or piece of furniture. Essentially, I leapt from one solid support to another. Even at night, the pain was so bad it disrupted my sleep, and I rarely felt rested. When it got even worse that summer, I had to crawl to the bathroom at night if needed. *What was happening to me*? My symptoms of PTSD continued, now coupled with random debilitating joint pain for which there was no treatment. My health was failing me, on top of everything else. I was worried and scared and alone. Now, more so than ever, I felt my freedom and independence floating away as terrifying, restricting physical prison walls closed in.

My forty-fifth college reunion was coming up in fall, and my friends were starting to e-mail each other about plans for the event. Emory and Henry College in southwest Virginia was an idyllic place to study, grow, and forge lasting bonds. We were a close-knit group, and I had not been to a homecoming since Mike died. I was hoping to go to this one, but with my current physical restraints, I did not think it would be possible. One of my sorority sisters who knew of my physical decline suggested I look into studying the mind-body connection. Linda told me her story of pain and healing. When her chronic back pain became unexplainable and no treatment seemed to help, her doctor advised her to read about TMS, as a possible alternative treatment. TMS originally stood for tension myositis syndrome and now has been expanded to the more inclusive phrase *the mind-body syndrome*, among others. Her pain receded in a matter of weeks, she canceled all scheduled PT sessions, and never needed one again. Finally, I had hope.

I dug right in and checked out books, websites, and endless testimonials of healing. I kept reading and kept digging. I learned that negative physical manifestations after emotional trauma are common. Within ten weeks of this revelation and constant study, I was pain-free and felt like myself again. Finally, something made sense. I was able to plow through the information, reading and reflecting, taking what seemed to fit, and leaving that which did not. Armed with greater respect, awareness, and understanding of how connected our bodies are with our minds and emotions, I rejoiced in my newfound physical freedom. I did not have to *do* anything. No meditation, no yoga, no doctor visits, no meds—just the information and knowledge gained from an actual explanation armed me with enough understanding to shift. There was no doubt in my mind that the suffering and the complicated grief I experienced after losing Mike was the stimulus for this painful and chronic condition. Elated to feel good and pain-free again, I made it to homecoming after all and immediately gave Linda a grateful hug. I walked all over campus with no problem and enjoyed the beloved tradition with my lifelong friends as never before.

Resources of every kind are available to explain what happens, but basically, it is the mind's way of diverting a person from focusing on deep-seated or psychological distress by creating physical pain or conditions that demand immediate attention. It provides distraction for a person allowing them to avoid facing or dealing with repressed psychological issues. But it is the avoidance of such issues that brings on the pain. Most of us do not have any trouble accepting the fact that blushing and goosebumps are a consequence of an emotional stimulus resulting in a physical manifestation. And we can usually relate to the undeniable rush of adrenaline when suddenly frightened. But to take that one step further and see how it might be relative to more acute bodily experiences is a leap of faith too great for many to consider. It does not happen overnight and may take weeks into months to internalize the concepts, and then some follow-up, but with sustained conscious effort to understand the powerful relationship between our minds and bodies, healing that is nothing short of miraculous is possible.

Another miracle was the blessing that no one was hurt during a traffic accident I survived. On my way to visit a friend, a woman slammed into my SUV as I initiated a left turn. She was on her phone, had been following too closely, and driving too fast. There was extensive damage to both vehicles. That led to weeks of anguish over the police reports, dealing with insurance to clear myself of blame, and getting the car repaired. Soon thereafter at the Honda dealership, I broke down and wept right there with the poor mechanic. I was trying my best to cope, but thoughts of Mike and what we had lost were always showing up when least expected. Being forced to make decisions about these issues concerning car repair and insurance, of which I was so unfamiliar, pushed all my emotional buttons. The sobering reality of my new normal, having to deal with everything by myself, was a steep step to make on the ladder climbing out of this hole. Why wasn't Mike here to handle this as usual? Why did he have to leave me so soon? How would I manage? I was left with so much more to do now, both his chores and mine. This was insult to injury. I struggled to contend.

My sobering new reality kept showing up, regurgitating thoughts of how different things used to be. Memories of Mike in his retirement job commuting for twelve years with FEMA surfaced, but pointed out a glaring difference. The girls were out of the house, in college or beyond, leaving me alone when he was deployed. But it was an aloneness far different from this new solitary confinement that I loathed. He was gone a lot then, and during those years, I fancied myself quite the independent woman. I felt I was handling household matters just fine, even in his absence. What I did not realize was how much he was contributing even from afar. I did not fully appreciate all he did on his few days home. And I did not realize before that just knowing he was there for me, no matter what his location, lifted me emotionally.

We were a couple, a team. I always said to people when he was gone during that time, that I was alone, but I was not lonely, and it was true. He might be away for two or three weeks at a time, then home again, then gone again. But it was a job he enjoyed, and we did not consider it a burdensome separation. Daily phone calls and e-mails kept us close. I often visited him on deployment, welcoming the interesting travel. It was the lifestyle we chose for that chunk of our lives. Best of all, I always knew he was coming home. I delighted in getting the house cleaned and cooking a familiar dish that made the kitchen smell scrumptious so that when he arrived and walked in the front door, he knew he was home. But this stillness and solitariness that engulfed me now was strikingly foreign. No longer part of a couple, no longer part of a team, I was alone, really alone. It was sheer torture. And it was a completely different experience than his being away on business. Not so independent now, are you? No phone calls or e-mails, and no need to clean the house or prepare his favorite meal. He is never coming home again.

As I endeavored to accept my new reality, I became aware of yet another troubling and unwelcome prediction for those in mourning. It was embedded within the general declaration that "grief never ends." In the early months, it was one of those things I read and heard then wondered about in my head and heart. But being too out of my head and heart to make any sense of it, I let it go. Now that I have had more time to digest it, I say emphatically that in my experience, this is a misnomer and warrants our scrutiny. For example, the Internet is filled with the following anonymous quote which begins: "Grief never ends…but it changes." It goes on to say that grief is not weakness or lack of faith but the price of love. Pretty words, but I find them unhelpful for mourners who may need some hope, and these are *not* words of hope. A similar sentiment can be found in a grief handbook that basically forewarns that grief takes years to process and, in some cases, will never be "got over." What a grim forecast for the already downtrodden! With all due respect to grief expert Elisabeth Kübler-Ross, she declares these haunting words, "The reality is that you will grieve forever."

*There seems to be no shortage
of life sentences being
handed out for grief prison.
And forever is a
long, long time.*

I have a graphic memory of hanging out in *grief prison* just doing my time when the warden stopped by. I am aware that he knows he has complete power over me and that I am at his mercy. He hands me an unexpected envelope with a smirk. I look at it suspiciously, and he says, "Go ahead, open it." It is a card of sorts, and on the front is the image of a clock with the pendulum swinging. It is ticktocking away, but there are no hands measuring the hours. Inside the card are these words:

*Grief never ends.
Some losses are never
"got over."
You will grieve forever.*

He turns to leave, then looks back at me with a wave and grunts, "Have a nice day."

I read the card again and pause, stunned at the weight of these words. "No!" I exclaim! I tear up the card in tiny bits and throw it to the wind out my cell window. No, I do not accept that as my truth. No, I do not believe in *never*. And no, you will not make that choice for me—I make my own choices.

Many subtle, insinuated messages are interwoven through traditional grief therapy. The words are not meant to hurt us, but they can and they do. If we take them to heart, they become part of our forward path, influenced forever by something that may not truly resonate with us at all. I take issue—I disagree. What happened to the concept that everyone grieves differently and in their own way? In my opinion, there really is no place for these sweeping negative statements that are delivered unilaterally to the grieving among us. In fact, grief can and does end for many people. Burdening the self with this foreboding threat that grief never ends will only keep us imprisoned. It may seem like it will never end when in the thick of it, but in fact, it *can* end, and over time, healing prevails. Just because the words have been uttered by some well-meaning soul, they are not necessarily true for you. For a person, weak and vulnerable, in a fresh grief, it can be genuinely detrimental to hear with some "authority" that this dire state will never end. To be told this will last "forever" is an unwarranted conviction.

Personally, I am certain that I am done with grieving for my parents. It was very painful at that time, but in no way am I still going through the process. More to the point perhaps, I do not feel I am still in active grief over my husband, Mike. As I write this now, years after losing him, I can say I did my time wrestling with the debilitating anguish of the *dark side*, and then I moved on. I miss him and think about him often and always will, but I am past the behavior, feelings, and life choices that could be categorized as grief. Each of us may choose to live without the ominous condemnation that "grief never ends." Those going through grief may choose to unburden their souls and lighten their loads; it is simply too heavy to carry the weight of grief forever!

Darth Vader has nothing on *grief*. They are both powerful and dark. They both threaten to bring us down and shake us up in ways we never dreamed possible. They persist in a cloud of misfortune and negativity that exudes an ominous feeling. I have experienced the *dark side of grief*. I have felt it when shrouded in black, as I wandered through a bleak midwinter. I have felt it when the power of suggestion dictates, "The third year is the worst" or "Grief never ends." I have felt it in the emotional amputation of being deemed single and alone again. I have felt it when the phrase "Life is meant to be shared" does not apply anymore. I have felt it in serious physical manifestations of emotional scars. I have felt it while staring out a window, seeing a neglected garden with no bluebirds.

But that is just the *dark side of grief*. I know that now. There is the other side, full of light and healing. There is a goodness in grief, and I found it. There are blessings in the darkness just waiting to be discovered. There are choices to be made. Darth Vader must reckon with the *force*, and *grief* must reckon with *love*.

2

Where Stars at Night Are Big and Bright

Star light, star bright
First star I see tonight
I wish I may, I wish I might
Have the wish I wish tonight.

The year 1971 came in with a bang! After lots of wishing on that first star of the night, my wishes were starting to come true. Within a few short months, I had graduated from college and soon after received this exciting news, "Congratulations! You have been selected for stewardess training at American Airlines!" After interviews, application forms, and weeks of waiting, the official acceptance letter arrived in the mail at last. I devoured the details about this exciting new job. In a few weeks, I would be leaving Williamsburg and be on my way to Dallas where American Airlines headquarters had recently moved from New York City. I would be starting in a new college, the Stewardess College as it was called, which hosted a new class of sixty candidates each week depending on the recruitment needs. I had earned a degree in elementary education from Emory and Henry College in Virginia, but I wanted to put that on the back burner for now. Unquestionably, being a stewardess sounded like a lot more fun than teaching third grade! I planned to fly for a couple of years for the experience and travel opportunities, having no idea which of my youthful wishes would come true—and which would not.

My family had lived in Williamsburg, Virginia for about six years, and we loved the small town, college town, colonial town atmosphere. I had an older brother, John, and a younger sister, Janine, and was content to be the middle child. The three of us had a good time in high school and made lifelong friends there. We were all active in various clubs and activities, and mine included student government and cheerleading. I particularly loved cheerleading—wearing the uniform, school spirit, pep rallies, and hearing the crowd join in as we shouted, "Victory, victory is our cry—V-I-C-T-O-R-Y!" Our basketball team even won the state championship in our sophomore year with a three-point shot on the final buzzer! When it comes to cheerleading a memorable game, it does not get any better than that! Like many girls at that time, I had a serious Annette Funicello and Sandra Dee wannabe thing going on. Cheerleading was as close as I could come to that squeaky clean, goody-two-shoes image, and I embraced it. But my biggest thrill came in my senior year when I was crowned homecoming queen at halftime of the season's biggest football game on a cold night in November. That is a cherished moment I will never forget.

Sadly, the fun and games ended at the close of my senior year when my parents became divorced, with all the disruption and messiness that implies. Our family was torn apart just as I left for college, which made the separation that much harder. Our parents

continued to have disagreements and diffi-
culties even after the divorce, which was bit-
ter and devastating to the three of us. My new
college friends helped me cope with the sadness of the divorce, but after graduation, my
old hometown did not feel like such a welcome place anymore. I was thrilled to have an
opportunity with American Airlines to start
fresh in a new location.

Material to review and memorize was
included along with detailed instructions
for what to bring to training. We would be
flown directly to our new base after graduation, so packing was important. Learning the
three-letter airport codes was first on the list
and included some obvious ones, but others
that did not make sense. For example, LAX
and DCA were easy, but how did ORD orig-
inate for Chicago? I learned that an aircraft
factory known as Orchard Place predated
O'Hare. It was later known as Orchard Field
when it became a commercial landing strip. I
had to confess, I already loved learning about
and preparing to become part of the explod-
ing airline industry.

Coffee, Tea or Me was a current bestseller, subtitled *The Uninhibited Memoirs of Two Airline Stewardesses*. The popularity of both the book and air travel was surging. The job was considered "glamorous," and the sky goddess image was part of the mystique they were selling. Most travelers then were businessmen, and the uniforms, makeup, and geisha girl-persona were promoted at least in part to keep them happy. I gobbled up each delicious tidbit in the book and savored the delightful possibilities. I lost ten pounds, said goodbye to life as I knew it, and embraced my new adventure.

The departure lounge at Dulles airport was the starting point for this new opportunity and, it seemed, my new life. I kissed my mom and sister goodbye, clinched my first-class boarding pass, and never looked back. I had only been on two flights in my young life, and as I walked down the jet bridge to the open door of the 707, I knew I was in the right place. The stewardess in first class greeted me and helped me stow my carry-on. Soon, another young woman about my age sat down next to me in the luxurious oversized seats, as we were offered champagne before takeoff. Not surprisingly, we were on the same nonstop trajectory to a new adventure. Brenda and I would become lifelong friends.

When we arrived in Dallas, we met a limo outside baggage claim as instructed for transportation to the American Airlines Stewardess College a.k.a. the Stew School. We climbed into the limo, and a girl in the front seat turned around flashing a big, beautiful smile and said to us in a thick southern accent, "Hi, I'm Ginger from Naaaashville." As we checked into the sprawling campus of the training facility, we were assigned rooms and roommates. Brenda, Ginger, and I would bunk together, and when we arrived at our suite, Peggy and Mary Beth were already unpacking.

Not long after, the pay phone in the hallway outside our room began to ring. Some guys in an apartment near Love Field in the singles area of Dallas had secured the number of these payphones in the Stew School. "Very clever," we had to admit. Someone answered it. We had not been in Dallas more than a few hours when we were accepting an invitation to be picked up at the front door at 7:00 p.m. by a bunch of complete strangers. All we knew was that we had been invited to a pool party with a band and kegs of beer, and it sounded like fun. Our first night in Dallas, and we were going to a party!

We got to the reception area downstairs and gathered at the large glass front doors. We noticed several other girls also waiting, having been contacted by the phones near their rooms on other floors of the dorm. What a system! Each week, a fresh batch of cute young ladies with stars in their eyes arrived, and these guys were working it. Soon, five or six cars pulled up, and the doors opened. Off we went, getting a great start to our new life, even if we did have to be back for the 11:00 p.m. curfew.

After the twenty-minute drive, we were invited into the apartment of the guy who drove us there. It was small talk and boring as we waited for the party to begin, but soon things picked up. The music started, and we moved out to the pool area and filled our plastic cups with beer. Darkness fell, and as the lights enhanced the party mood around the pool, more and more apartment dwellers came out to join us and meet this week's new girls. Now *this* was a party.

Then came the moment I will never forget. Three guys arrived about the time we were thinking we should be asking our driver to take us back. They had not been connected to the party organizers but lived in the apartments and were just checking out the scene. They approached Mary Beth, Ginger, and me and struck up a conversation. One was Tommy Joe, with a good Southern name and a sweet smile. The other one was Danny, cute and full of laughs. The third was tall and blond with sparkling blue eyes, and he only seemed to be interested in me. Time stood still as we talked and laughed with our eyes locked on each other. It felt like magic, when suddenly he stepped back and grabbed his chest with both hands over his heart and declared to all within earshot, "I'm in *love*!"

And that was our beginning, and that was *my* Mike.

It was late. He asked if he could take me back to the Stew Zoo (another nickname for the school), and I accepted. We were getting close to curfew time, and I knew the consequences could be severe—and on the first night no less! We had been told that we could be sent home for the smallest offense and that there were ten applicants waiting for each of the jobs we had been offered. Mike drove too fast in his blue Ford Mustang Mach I, and he got me there, just *after* the big swinging gates across the entry road had been closed and locked! We jumped out of the car and ran toward the gate pleading. The custodian was just walking away, and we called to him. "Please let me in," I begged. He turned around and paused, then showed us mercy. I was never late for curfew again.

Monday arrived, and the six-week training began. It was intense and intimidating. My fellow trainees were all female, smart, in great shape, and one prettier than the next. The code of conduct was strict, and not everyone made it. It was clear management would not hesitate to send home a "troublemaker" or anyone who failed to comply. A

disappearing act during lunch was the pre-
ferred method of removal. After morning
classes, the offending party would be asked to
meet her supervisor who would inform them
they were going home. Someone would help
them hurriedly pack then load them into a
limo back to Love Field. By the time others
returned from lunch, they were long gone,
and no trace was to be found of their former
roommate or any of her belongings. Not even
a goodbye… That put the fear in everyone.
We all wondered, "Am I next?"

Mike called me on the dorm pay phone,
and it took my breath away when I heard his
sweet Southern accent. He planned a fun date
or outing for us every weekend and sometimes a midweek visit as well. It was exciting
to be with him and get to know him. I wondered where it would go. He was finishing his
thesis at North Texas, would graduate soon,
then send out résumés in the Dallas area. We
both had a lot going on but made time for
each other.

A variety of manuals was presented
during class, and the sheer volume of data
seemed daunting. They included everything

from the location of emergency equipment on the various airplanes we might fly, to learning CPR, to how to serve "liquor and dinner" to one hundred passengers in less than an hour. Practicing how to direct an evacuation in case of an emergency landing was particularly critical. Simulators of the various planes provided a realistic setting. Noises blared, "smoke" puffed out of walls, and darkness fell, allowing the emergency light system to activate. Fellow students pretended to be passengers as one by one we were called upon to demonstrate an evacuation in real-time panic mode, shouting all the mandated commands. The finale was to open that formidable airplane door and scream "Jump! Jump! Jump!" as our classmates obediently obliged.

Our appearance was important back in the seventies. We were subjected to regular grooming checks including a weigh-in, followed by a supervisor measuring our hips and waists with a plastic tape. The numbers were recorded, and we could not exceed the limits—or else. The cafeteria food was pretty good, and being away from home and under so much stress, there was the temptation to allow food to soothe the unsettled soul. Warm freshly baked cookies were served at an evening meeting or class, filling the air with chocolaty goodness, but we were reluctant to indulge, well aware of the consequences.

Grooming sessions were held on how to gracefully sit and stand, how to walk in heels, and how to don and remove a jacket in the proper way. Classes on how to apply makeup and nail polish included an introduction to fake eyelashes. They were encouraged, for sale in the lobby shop, and we were taught how to apply them. The "Charm Farm" more than earned its name! Exact guidelines were provided on both the minimum and maximum height of our navy blue heels. No flats allowed! When in uniform, earrings could be only silver, gold, red, white, or blue—studs only, no dangles. Necklaces could not be visible, and only simple bracelets were tolerated.

Finally, we were fitted for our uniforms, which gave us hope. In the last weeks we were given a "makeover," implying that we still needed a lot of help. Professional hairstylists cut and colored our hair followed by a team of makeup artists who applied full makeup with advice on colors for eye shadow, lipstick, and nail polish. An official individual graduation photo was taken in uniform at the end of the makeover day. We were being prepared to be the best we could be, and no wonder some likened the experience to that of a bygone finishing school.

There was a strong comradery building, and we felt mutual support within our sisterhood. Six fast-paced stressful weeks were taking their toll. Anxiety and homesickness were widespread. "Leaving on a Jet Plane," written by John Denver and performed by Peter, Paul and Mary was high on the charts and became our unofficial theme song. Heard often, it pushed some buttons. Several were as young as twenty, and this was their first time away from home. Some had left a love behind. The haunting lyrics heightened their emotions and made them question their decision to fly. "Oh babe, I hate to go…"

I, on the other hand, was having the time of my life! Weekends with Mike were a delight. A whirlwind of dating continued as we saw each other as often as possible. Fancy dinners with dancing in landmark restaurants to impress me were working. I was introduced to Six Flags amusement park where he proudly won a big teddy bear for me at the arcade. He loved Dallas, and he loved showing it off to me. His kisses were irresistible, and in his strong arms, I felt safe. Our sweet talk was serious, but we were facing a separation that could not be avoided. I had just learned I would be based in New York City for at least six months and possibly more. He was starting to say things about our future together, and I questioned how he could be so sure. He spoke softly, "Just give me a chance to prove it to you."

The drills, tests, and deadlines were complete, and graduation day arrived. We were so proud to officially wear our uniforms for the first time. Silver wings were ceremoniously pinned on to our uniform by our supervisor. A tall winding staircase in the grand hall was the site of the class group graduation photo with the fifty of us who made it all the way. A reception followed with lots of celebration;

then, we packed our bags and left for our new bases. We were ready for takeoff!

Brenda, Ginger, Peggy, Mary Beth, and I were roommates once again—this time in a small, one-bedroom, furnished apartment on the upper East Side. We had four twin beds lined up in the one bedroom, and if by some chance all five of us were home, someone slept on the sofa in the small living room. We were all flying as much as possible to earn money and pay the bills. Walking the halls to our apartment, we could hear Rod Stewart's "Wake Up Maggie" playing on the radio along with some favorite Carole King. It was fun and exciting, and we forged a strong bond. None of us were city girls, and we could hardly believe we were living in Manhattan and referring to it as "the city." Attending Broadway matinees on our days off and window shopping at Bloomingdale's and Saks Fifth Avenue felt like a dream. Splurging one night, we feasted with a memorable dinner at Mama Leone's. But it was not all glamour. I remember with disgust that we were advised by the super in our apartment building to keep the toilet lid down at all times and put a brick on top of it at night to keep rats from coming up from the sewer.

Eager to see Mike as much as possible, I would sweet-talk crew schedule into giving me trips with long Dallas layovers. They teased me about treating them like a travel agency, then helped me out if they could. An abundance of tender love letters, phone calls, and a few layovers each month kept us close. We knew we were falling in love. I put in for a transfer to Dallas, and it came through in March.

Mike still lived with Tommy Joe in the apartment where we met almost a year ago. I got an apartment nearby with a six-month lease, sharing it with a stewardess from my class. DFW was being built then and had not yet opened, so we were flying out of Love Field, which seemed appropriate. We knew it was serious, and within weeks, he bought me an engagement ring and asked me to marry him. We planned a fall wedding. He would soon be my husband and eligible to share my airline passes. The travel opportunities were impressive, really opening up the world for us, and we could not wait to get started. "Marry Me—Fly Free" was a popular poster of the day, featuring some not-so-glamorous stewardesses of early flight days. We joked about that, but we knew we did not need that perk because we were so in love and overflowing with optimism about our future.

As our engagement progressed, we continued to learn more and more about each other. My fiancé was a loving man, a person of high character, and someone I truly admired. He was from a small town in Mississippi near Hattiesburg, where he lived most of his young life. A skinny six-foot, five-inch teen, he played basketball in high school and earned the nickname "Stork." He was elected president of the senior class and president of the student government in the same year. He attained the distinction of being the youngest boy in the history of Mississippi at that time to receive the rank of Eagle Scout at age thirteen. He earned a coveted admission to the Air Force Academy after high school but dropped out during his freshman year when

Gail Norwood

his forty-five-year-old father died suddenly
of lung cancer, leaving his mother to care for
four children still at home. Later he told me
that leaving the academy was the biggest mis-
take of his life. But he said at that time, he
just could not leave his family in that crisis
without coming home to help.

After a few years, he joined the army.
Vietnam was raging, and he felt called to do
his part. In fact, he went above and beyond
doing his part. He proudly earned a Green
Beret. This was no small feat, as Barry Sadler
describes in his popular ballad of 1966. The
training was lengthy and intense and took
place at Fort Bragg, North Carolina. He told
stories about being dropped from a helicop-
ter into Pisgah National Forest in western
North Carolina in the cold of winter for survival training and about how he jumped out
of several "perfectly good airplanes." Proud to
serve with his Special Forces team, he fought
in Vietnam for six terrifying months. Upon
returning from duty, when he got off the
plane with his fellow soldiers, angry protes-
tors in the San Francisco airport threw tomatoes at them and shouted obscenities. His

time in service was intense, and although he did not talk about it, his nightmares continued for years.

It was after returning from Vietnam that he finished his undergrad, then earned a master's degree in Municipal Government. That same spring before his graduation, we met and fell in love. He was offered an impressive job that grew from an internship with the City of Dallas, and I settled into flying out of Love Field, then soon thereafter, moved to DFW when it opened. Life had taken him from Mississippi to Colorado Springs, to Fort Bragg, to Vietnam, to Dallas, Texas. And life had taken me from Williamsburg and Emory, Virginia, straight to Dallas where our two paths happily intersected at a random pool party on a warm spring night. Life had brought us together, and the timing was perfect. Hopeful words I had spoken earlier came to mind and brought up a deep satisfying smile, "I wish I may, I wish I might, have the wish I wish tonight."

I had been raised Catholic, and we would have a "mixed marriage" as it was called at that time, joining a Catholic and a non-Catholic in the sacrament of matrimony. Mike was raised in the Baptist faith but would comply with the requirements for our wedding, also officially agreeing to allow me to raise our children as Catholics by signing the required forms. He willingly complied, but he never felt comfortable with Catholicism and never attended church with me or our eventual family. These were choices we made at the time of our marriage, not realizing the implications they would have on our relationship and our family as time wore on. We wanted to be together, and we would work through anything that threatened to get in the way.

We were married on a perfect fall day in October 1972 in my hometown of Williamsburg. Our wedding, simple but elegant, was held in the local Catholic church my family had attended, followed by a classic champagne reception in the East Lounge of the Williamsburg Inn. My father walked me down the aisle, and he and my mother were on their best behavior that day, but the tension between them was undeniable. My father had remarried, but his new wife was not welcome at our wedding, according to my mother. My mom and dad stood together on the altar for the group family wedding photos and smiled for the camera like one big happy family. These were difficult times for my parents, and I know they were trying to make the best of it, but along with my wedding vows that day, I offered up an ardent prayer to God that Mike and I would never have to suffer through a divorce.

Both my parents thought the world of Mike, and much of the conversation and attention was centered on him and his family who were all in attendance. We were surrounded by our families and dear friends and were over the moon to become husband and wife. The next morning, we left on our weeklong honeymoon to Bluebeard's Castle in Saint Thomas, Virgin Islands, our hearts bursting with love and anticipation of our lives together. Two weeks earlier, I had turned twenty-two, and he was twenty-seven. Our newlywed status was divine, but we were both eager to return to Dallas, settle into our new apartment, and start living our dream.

It was exciting and trendy to live in Dallas in the early seventies, with the success and phenomena of the Dallas Cowboys and the popularity of the TV series *Dallas*, with its spicy shenanigans at Southfork Ranch. "Who shot JR?" was the question of the day. But for me, living there was just temporary. I missed the east coast where my family remained, and I never felt at home in Texas. Mike understood, admitting to his own fondness for Virginia and the Carolinas, promising we would move back there "in a few years." But until then, we looked forward to traveling as much as possible and starting a family.

Our first daughter was born in 1976, a bicentennial baby. We named her Mary Evelyn in honor of both grandmothers, as she was the first born on either side. Almost four years later, we joyfully welcomed baby Amy, completing our family. We adored our little girls and felt so blessed to have them in our lives. Mike was an attentive and loving father, and these early years for our family were precious. I attended St. Rita Catholic Church in a nearby neighborhood and with Mike's blessing enrolled the girls into St. Rita School as they became of age. He did not attend mass with us but would come to celebrate first communion or other special occasions. Years passed, filled with the usual progressions of raising a family and managing careers. Things were good but not without the usual ups and downs that life presents.

My flying career continued, and when we became parents, I chose to fly twelve all-nighters or turnarounds each month. Otherwise, I would be gone on two- or three-day trips, but this way, I could be home part of every day or night. I was exhausted much of the time, but for a full-time working mother, I was able to be home with my daughters a lot, which is what I wanted. I started a practice to which I was true until the day of retirement. I wanted so much to return to my growing family and could not dismiss the possibility that some fateful event might take me away from them. It was the reality of my job. As I strapped into my jump seat for each takeoff and landing, I would fervently offer a prayer. When the moment came for liftoff or touchdown when most accidents happen, I closed my eyes and begged, "Dear God, go with us, and bring me safely home." And He always did.

Being a mother was, for me, an ineffable joy. I even loved being pregnant and the moment each of them first moved inside me was a thrill unlike no other. Nursing my new babies was completely satisfying and an extension of the closeness we felt during gestation. Decorating their nurseries was such fun, and I watched with wonder as they grew into toddlers, then precious little girls. My sewing skills came in handy as I dressed them in matching outfits and made little clothes for their dolls. I piddled around with a few plants in containers to brighten the backyard, happily learned how to cook for my young family, and embraced the whole domestic goddess persona. Motherhood agreed with me later as I dutifully arranged piano, gymnastic, and dance lessons. I became their Girl Scout troop leader when Mary Evelyn was in kindergarten, continuing as leader of one troop or the other off and on for ten years. A friend gave me a framed cross-stitch as a baby gift, featuring a verse from a poem written by Ruth Hulburt Hamilton. The words proclaimed this truth and became my motto:

> Cooking and cleaning
> can wait till tomorrow
> For babies grow up, I've
> learned to my sorrow,
> So settle down cobwebs,
> and dust go to sleep—
> I'm rocking my baby,
> and babies don't keep.

On some rare occasions, I was away on a two- or three-day trip, and while I would miss Mike and the girls, I appreciated the many special moments afforded me. More than once, the Aurora Borealis or the Northern Lights were visible on an all-nighter, and the cockpit would invite us up, one at a time for the show. I had to pinch myself to realize I was thirty thousand feet in the sky witnessing this incredible natural light display, up close and personal. Another time we flew over Mount St. Helens during the volcanic eruption and marveled at the privilege of seeing this rare spectacle. Perhaps my most meaningful trip was returning a Vietnam prisoner of war to his hometown in Little Rock, Arkansas. He was sitting in first class in full uniform with only one other passenger. I was working that cabin and tried to chat with him, but he was too nervous to talk. We arrived and first deplaned all the other passengers using the mobile stairway instead of a jet bridge. The tarmac below was a sea of faces waiting to greet this man, their long-lost local hero. The press was there with TV cameras, and his anxious family gathered at the bottom of the stairs. It was time. He got up his courage, stepped out of the airplane door, and paused. The crowd erupted into cheers and shouts as he stood there in salute. God knows what this soldier had been through all those years, but at last, he was home.

I cannot even begin to count the number of celebrities that were on my flights, but on a month of double Nashville turnarounds out of Dallas, well you can just imagine: Willie Nelson, Dolly Parton, Glen Campbell, Charlie Pride, even Roy Rogers and Dale Evans of *The Roy Rogers Show*! Too many to count, but it added an element of interest and excitement to our otherwise monotonous days. I kept a little collection of all my autographs, and if it was someone like Tom Landry or Pete Rose, I had them address it to Mike instead of me. My best ever superstar passenger was Mother Teresa, in coach of course. I do not remember what city we were flying to or from, but to witness the awe of her presence was profound. I sat next to her for a moment to say hello, and she signed her autograph to me with the words, "Peace begins with a smile."

Working with an airline as large as American allowed me to develop a global perspective and a valuable exposure to our human diversity that I was able to pass along to our girls. People from so many other cultures were part of my life, from both my fellow employees to the passengers. I gained a keener view of the world in the early years with interesting layovers, in such places as

Acapulco, San Francisco, Honolulu, Toronto, and the Caribbean just to name a few. Of course, there were several less-exciting cities thrown in, but they all had something to offer. Later, when our daughters were older and I joined the international ranks, I got to spend lots of time in Paris, London, and Frankfurt, which I dearly loved. Closer to home, because of my very affordable airline passes, Mike and I were able to plan amazing family trips and provide enriching experiences for our girls. Disney World was one of our early adventures followed by San Antonio, Hawaii, Cancun, an Alaskan cruise, and others. When they were older, we crossed the pond to Belgium, France, and England. I could say I've looked at clouds from both sides now, and what a ride!

Big D was a fine place to start our family. We began with a small starter home and then graduated to one larger and Texas style, complete with a pool and a fenced backyard. A pool was part of the Dallas lifestyle and helped us survive the torturous summers. It was the center of our family activities during the warm months, and we often hosted our

girls with neighborhood kids practicing syn-
chronized swimming routines, doing a can-
nonball off the low board, and endlessly
shouting "Marco" and "Polo." No longer a
skinny teenager, Mike had bulked up after
his military training, followed by years at the
gym. He could easily lift the girls to his broad
shoulders then go running into the deep end
of the pool with a big splash to squeals of
delight. After their bedtime, we would often
return to the pool under an evening sky,
watching legendary stars so big and bright.
We played music and talked as we rested in
the poolside chaise lounges, sipping a glass of
wine, and succumbing to the temptation of a
goodnight skinny dip.

A bonus of the second house was that it
provided a perfect place in the front room for
our baby grand piano. As a child in Paris, my
mother took lessons on that same piano. The
hand-carved rosewood music stand proudly
stated that that the maker was Gaveau of
Paris. The piano survived a trip in the belly
of an ocean liner across the Atlantic when my
parents moved to the States after meeting and
marrying in Paris just after the war. My sis-

ter and I took lessons on this beauty as we admired our mom for her advanced musical skills.

Years later after Mike and I married, when my mother was downsizing, we had the opportunity to become the new proud owners. It was not only a musical instrument but also a handsome feature in our home. We flew to Virginia, rented a U-Haul, and drove the new "baby" all the way to Dallas. It was in disrepair with much of the beautiful rosewood veneer peeling off. For Christmas that year, Mike presented me with the cash to get the estimated repairs done, likely the best gift ever. It was two years in the shop, but when finished, it looked like new. We had the sounding board replaced and added new strings. Our girls started taking lessons at age four, filling the house with their daily practices as they learned the joy of making music.

With its close proximity to St. Rita Church, the girls could ride their bikes to school from our new house. Off they would go each morning in their green and navy-blue parochial school uniforms with a crisp white collared shirt and classic saddle shoes.

Our family blossomed in this house, including a deepening bond between Mike and me as we embraced our family and each other. His career with the City of Dallas was taking off and mine with American Airlines was steady and satisfying. By all accounts, everything seemed fine, but in truth, an underlying issue was festering. Something threatened to disrupt the calm, and it was deep and real. Usually the business of daily life took precedence and kept us from facing it head-on. The elephant in the room was swept under the rug once again. And that is not easy to do.

3

The Southern Part of Heaven

On his deathbed Dr. Kluttz
queried Parson Moss
about what Heaven
might be like.
Moss replied, "I believe
Heaven must be a lot like
Chapel Hill in the spring."

—From "The Southern
Part of Heaven"

by William Meade Prince

*A*fter almost nineteen years in Dallas, I
acknowledged a deepening frustration that

was morphing into resentment at still living here with no plans in sight to move back east. The elephant in the room wore a ten-gallon hat and four western boots with pointed toes. The cowboy culture, the unrelenting heat and exhausting length of a southwestern summer, the predictably flat terrain with short trees and a whole lot of sky—all so Texas and all so *not me*.

A common phrase of the day popularized by the artwork of Mary Engelbreit proclaimed, "Bloom where you are planted." I heard it, and I got the message. I wondered what was wrong with me to acknowledge feelings within that did not support this seemingly solid piece of advice. It is a nice message about making the best of wherever one is in this life, but it did not apply to me in this situation. By all accounts, my life in Dallas was enviable. I had my beloved family, a home of which I was proud, a job I enjoyed, and a nurturing social circle. But deep down, I was consumed with the desire to be doing all these things and living this same life in the southeast instead of here in Texas.

I knew my feelings were authentic and deserved to be recognized. "To thine own self be true" and all that. This was the agreement Mike and I made before we were ever married, and it could not be ignored. My limited gardening knowledge supported questioning the validity of the phrase about where to bloom. If there is one thing true for Mother Nature, it is that planting things in the right place makes all the difference. Just as in real estate, it is location, location, location. Put a zinnia in the shade, and you are not going to get much back, but move it to a sunny bed and get out of the way! Put a gorgeous lime green hosta in full sun, and it is going to burn up and crisp on the edges. It is a law of nature and not one to be contested. Just like city folk not adjusting well to country life, it is also true that country folk may feel out of place in the city. No, everything does *not* bloom where it is planted. I had been planted in Dallas, Texas, and I was not blooming. And because I was not blooming, I knew I could not be my best for my husband and children—or myself.

Our lives in Dallas had been busy and full, rich with the trials and satisfactions of raising a young family. But for me at least, it had always been a temporary stop on the way home. Mike always knew this and remembered his promise to me from many years ago. He knew we had never intended to raise our kids in Dallas, but they were now in sixth and tenth grade, and time was running out. I had taken Mike's promise to heart and lived with the anticipation of its fulfillment all these years, but his career with City of Dallas kept advancing, and he felt it unwise to leave. I knew changing careers was not easy but nearly twenty years had passed, and I had been patient. With Mary Evelyn starting high school, something set off a thunderous alarm in my heart. There was no denying that big old cowboy elephant just kept coming in the room and would not budge.

Then, as so often occurs in life, just when we think we cannot go on, something happens. Mike heard the news first and came quickly to tell me. He was dressing for work, listening to his favorite radio station KVIL, as he did each morning. I was making breakfast for the girls when he rushed into the kitchen clinching a towel around his waist, with a toothbrush in his other hand and just a vestige of toothpaste still on his lips. "American just announced the opening of a new crew base and hub in Raleigh!" he exclaimed excitedly. I was stunned. I stood there in disbelief and could not speak. "I just heard it on the radio," he said. "There is no date yet, but it is in the works."

Our lives changed at that very moment. All the years of wondering how it would come to pass could now be put to rest. All the years of being unsettled with the unresolved anticipation of something yet to come would haunt us no more. All the years of waiting were coming to an end. We never saw that elephant again.

Mike and I both knew this was our chance. He was open to the idea from the start but at first could not quite see how all the pieces would fall into place. There was still his job to consider. I was energized with the possibility and became increasingly convinced this was the answer to our prayers. I would move heaven and earth to get the wheels in motion to make this dream come true. We had heard rumors to this effect for about a year, but life in the airline industry is one rumor after the other, none to be trusted until they become official. But now it *was* official! I happily cut out newspaper articles with the headlines and all the details. Notices were sent out in company mail. The new crew base would open in a few months, and applications for transfers would be accepted soon. Lyrics from "Carolina in My Mind" by Chapel Hill native James Taylor became my mantra. The words rang joyfully in my head, as I realized with great satisfaction that our new home would be that beautiful place about which he sang so lovingly.

Our plans started to evolve. Mike wanted the girls and me to go ahead with the move, and he would join us as soon as he could. I objected and said we would not go until we could all go together, but he declared it was less pressure on him this way, and he insisted. I could not imagine being separated from him after spending nearly every day together for the last twenty years, but this was a means to an end. An end I believed in and longed for. It was stressful with all the emotions, the sudden need to sell our Dallas home and look for a new one in Carolina. Add to this the uncertainty of Mike's new job and when things might be settled down again. One day, I came home from errands, and on the kitchen counter lay a single red rose with a note nearby. In it, Mike said, "I know this has been hard on you. I never knew it would take so long. You are the love of my life, and we will make this work."

This was happening! We had been talking about it for years, and the girls knew a move was imminent, so it was in no way a shock to them. It was almost more of a relief, a feeling of fulfillment, of "Let's get on with it if we're going!" I was quickly awarded a transfer from DFW to RDU, and it would be effective early in the new year. At least one of us would have a job there, and we could get the girls enrolled in school. It was harder for Mary Evelyn being in the tenth grade to leave the friends she had been with since kindergarten, but thankfully, Amy did not seem to skip a beat.

The plan was for Mike to commute for a while until he could find a job locally. I would fly out of the airport in Raleigh, but we chose to settle in nearby Chapel Hill, our own "Southern Part of Heaven." We were attracted by its charming small-town nature, the legendary basketball seasons, and other opportunities from hometown University of North Carolina, and especially its reputation for exceptional public school systems. We had a rush of farewell parties in Dallas, and I sent forget-me-not thank-you notes. These were good and solid friends, and we would all miss them, but this train had left the station.

We bought a beautiful traditional house on two acres just outside town, and it would become our dream home for decades. We celebrated our twentieth wedding anniversary that year, and Mike gave me the perfect gift: a sapphire and diamond bracelet, signifying the Carolina blue that was so ever-present in our new world. Neither of us was happy about him having to commute or for us to live apart during the week, but we were convinced it was a good move for our family, and this seemed like an opportunity that otherwise had not presented itself. He called it a "quality of life change." It just felt right. He had made good on his promise, and for that, I loved him even more.

It was a challenging transition for our family, but in the end, it was worth it. While in Dallas, we had faithfully followed the Duke-UNC basketball rivalry for years and knew the coaches' and most of the players' names. Now here we were in the middle of "March Madness" and loving it! The Tarheels won a national championship in 1993 soon after we arrived. The girls joined classmates and friends as locals and throngs of UNC students swarmed Franklin Street for the exciting celebration.

Adjusting to the new and different schools went as expected for our daughters—a few bumps and turns but overall satisfactory. Unlike the private schools in Dallas, Chapel Hill was a more diverse community with lots of international families working at UNC or Duke, making for a melting pot mix of middle and high school students. They even offered the international high school diploma due to the demand. I enjoyed flying out of RDU, still choosing turnarounds that allowed me to be home at night. The three of us attended the local Catholic church in town, and Mike remained on the outside, as it had been in Dallas. Mike's commute was tedious but the price we would pay for our new lifestyle. Weekends together were the highlight of our week as we explored our new hometown, and we remained a close and happy family.

A few months after we settled in, the City of Dallas announced an early-out plan based on a combination of age and years of service. Mike would qualify for the generous lifetime settlement in just over four years. It seemed unfathomable that his commute could continue that long, as we all desperately wanted him to find a job in Carolina soon so we could be together again in our new home and our new town. We had thought it might take a few months, maybe a year tops, but then, this new twist developed. Four years seemed like an interminable amount of time, but the bonus was a sweet prize at the finish line. We had to think about it as part of his job and that he just traveled a lot, like thousands of people do for a living. It was not what we wanted, but it was tolerable. Mike had plenty of vacation time built up, and we were often together for longer than just a weekend, making time for trips and family visits.

We all settled into our routine of work, school, and daily life, and a couple of years flew by. Our monotonous routine was shattered when on an annual checkup with my new internist, it was discovered that my platelets were three times the normal range. The test was repeated, but it revealed the same results. The doctor acted concerned and did not know the root cause. I told Mike right away, but we kept it from the girls for now, until we knew more. I was sent to a specialist as the platelets kept rising with every blood sample. This doctor told me it could be the early stages of leukemia, and they would soon start me on interferon, a drug known for its flu-like side effects, including fatigue and nausea. He predicted I would remain on interferon for as long as I might live.

I was completely shocked, in disbelief, and absolutely paralyzed with fear. We had finally made this monumental move to North Carolina, so dear to my heart, and now my health threatened to sabotage the happily ever after, even before Mike joined us full time. The girls still did not know. Emotionally, I could hardly manage my own thoughts of fear, and I could not risk having the girls upset and worried about me. I just would not be able to handle it, especially without Mike home on weekdays.

While waiting for another consultation, an option for a change in our medical insurance became available. As many companies were doing in the early nineties, American had switched our company insurance plan to an HMO, limiting our choice of doctors. But this proposed adjustment would allow us the option to change providers and be able to see any doctor of our choice. Instead of being limited to the HMO doctors, we could avail ourselves of all the medical muscle of the combined staff at nearby UNC and Duke Medical Centers. Mike and I decided to take advantage of this opportunity, and we completed the new enrollment package. We had to wait a couple of miserable months for the new insurance to take effect, but we knew it was worth it. And it seemed to take two or three weeks between this consultation or that new test. Would this waiting ever come to an end?

Meanwhile, my imagination was running wild with fear. Our girls still did not know and probably wondered why I was acting so cranky and depressed. All I could think about was them and Mike and our future, or lack thereof. I was only forty-four. Would I survive to feel the joy of Mike joining us full time in North Carolina after so many long years of waiting? Would I even get to finish raising my daughters? Would I be there to see them graduate from college and help them plan their weddings? Would I be blessed to meet and hold my future grandchildren? Oh Lord, please, this cannot be happening!

The time finally arrived for us to move forward, and Mike arranged to come home early and be with me as we saw the specialist in the UNC hematology department. Mike had been doing some research of excessive platelets while in Dallas and failed miserably at pretending he was not worried. The appointment was early in the day, so the girls were both in school. Mike and I were admitted to the examination room, and I was so scared I thought I would faint. I could not even sit; I was pacing. This was it. If this doctor also diagnosed me with early-stage leukemia, then we knew there was not much hope.

Dr. Berkowitz entered, saw my wet face, and sensed our panic. The first thing he said was "Leukemia is very rare." Instead, he told us this is very likely a case of essential thrombocytosis, which is a benign, chronic blood disorder but *not* leukemia. Even hearing about this possible alternative felt so encouraging. The HMO doctors never mentioned any such hypothesis. More tests were ordered, but to rule out leukemia decisively, a bone marrow aspiration and biopsy was required to test bone marrow cells and chromosomes. On subsequent visits, Dr. Berkowitz continued to reassure me that until we had more test results, there was no reason to assume leukemia. I was terrified, but we would soon know the truth. My whole life and the lives of my family were all in the balance.

Again, Mike arranged to be in town for the procedure, and we made up some story about why he was home midweek. It was spring break, and the girls had been invited to the beach with some friends, which was perfect timing. They would be gone about five days. Mike was with me in the hospital room after we checked in, trying to calm me down and reassure me. He was asked to leave when the doctor entered to begin the aspiration. The procedure was extremely painful and difficult to perform. I was given only a local anesthetic. The first try was unsuccessful, and the doctor apologized but succeeded the second time, ending the ordeal. I was moved to a recovery room where Mike joined me, and we waited together to learn the life-giving or life-changing results. Hours later, Dr. Berkowitz came in with the news—the tests did *not* indicate leukemia! I was still in pain, but I did not care. I was going to be okay! Mike and I were consumed by joy and gratitude for a new chance at life! It was confirmed that I had the blood disorder Dr. Berkowitz mentioned earlier, which caused excessive production of platelets, but "essentially," that was all. I now had enough platelets for six people, but I did not care—no leukemia!

Unusual and unpredictable clotting was the main complication with thrombocytosis, and it showed up on day one. The site of the bone marrow aspiration on my back would not quit bleeding. Hours in that recovery room showed little improvement. By day's end, another team of hematologists was called in to try to stop the bleeding with advanced measures. They finally achieved some success, and I was admitted to the hospital for observation overnight. Mike came to visit me the next day, and we were overjoyed at the positive test results. They kept me one more night; then Mike brought me home for some TLC. My back was very sore, and walking was difficult even with the pain meds. Our girls would return from the beach trip in a few days giving me a chance to rest and recover a little more before they arrived.

The wound in my spine had healed satisfactorily by the time our daughters were back in Chapel Hill, all tanned and oblivious to our crisis. I suggested going for a walk with them the next day, something we often did especially when we wanted to talk. It took some nerve, but I finally revealed the progression of the last four months and what their dad and I had endured as we went through the motions of ruling out this life-threatening disease. They were instantly furious! They could not believe I had "treated them like children" by not sharing these concerns until now. I understood their anger and expected nothing less. I tried to explain to them, that I did it not only to protect them from worry but also for my own peace of mind. I tried to explain that if they had known, they would have suffered through it with me, and to witness that would cause me even more pain and duress. I intended to spare us all from that added burden.

Another consideration was that during this last semester of high school for Mary Evelyn, she was busy finalizing her college choice and overflowing with excitement about receiving a substantial scholarship to her first-choice school, University of Georgia in Athens. I worried that if she knew about my medical uncertainty, she may question the wisdom of her leaving home in fall, especially since Mike was still commuting. Would she feel responsible to stay, not wanting to leave Amy to deal with it alone? Or worse yet, what if she pulled something like her father, dropping out of the Air Force Academy in his freshman year when his father became ill? What if somehow all this caused her to forfeit her scholarship and her freshman year? What if she decided not to go at all but to stay home to care for me? She had worked so hard to do well in school, and she *had* done well, and now she was reaping the benefits. I could not take a chance on having my uncertain situation trip her up at this point. Of course, they were mad at me—at us—for a long time, but that was okay. They were not mothers yet and did not know the extent to which mothers will go to protect their children. One day they would understand.

Months and years wore on, then finally with great celebration, we welcomed Mike home after exactly four years, four months, and twelve days. *Yes*, we were counting! He rented a truck in Dallas and packed things from his apartment there, then picked me up at DFW as I arrived from my flight to meet him. I jumped in the truck with a huge smile on my face, slammed the door shut, and proclaimed, "Let's go home!" And there it was at last: Dallas, in my rearview mirror.

We drove to North Carolina ceremoniously, taking a few days to enjoy the trip. It had been a long time coming, and we both felt deeply grateful about the transition we were finally able to achieve. Our family was reunited, and it felt so good. What jubilation! Satisfied with our mutual decision and the culmination of our efforts, we turned the page to an exciting new chapter in our lives. We made it to Carolina, and not just in our minds.

That same year, I took an early-out package and retired from American Airlines after twenty-five years of flying. The offer was too good to refuse, and I had another life waiting for me. My family, my garden, my new home, and my church received all my energy and attention. My real love turned out to be working outside trying to tame the former farmland acreage into an ornamental garden. It would become the garden of my dreams, of our dreams—a show garden.

Mike did the heavy lifting with the tiller and his chain saw, removing trees and debris while I planned the beds and paths. It took years but kept evolving into something remarkable and more beautiful than we ever expected. After lots of clearing was accomplished, hardscaping was added for structure and texture. We built a brick terrace in the back, adding numerous gravel paths inviting exploration. A hammock, firepit, and various benches placed strategically provided interest. But the heart of the garden was a colonial gazebo seated in a cleared area of the woodland. Set on a beautiful piece of land with an incredible halo of dogwoods in place, the structure fit perfectly, adding a magical charm. An exact replica of the gazebo at the Benjamin Waller House from my hometown Williamsburg, it became the crown jewel and centerpiece of our garden.

I joined the Chapel Hill Garden Club and soon became president for a couple of years, immersing myself in this delightful hobby. My little bit of earth nurtured my soul as I nurtured it in return. The lectures at the meetings helped train me as I learned what plants did well locally. I graduated to the master gardener course through the extension service and learned even more. Like my garden, I was in full bloom! New friendships with other gardeners came happily, with an abundance of pass-along plants to get me started. And like my new plants, I was putting down deep, long-lasting roots in a place where I felt indigenous. Most gifts to me from Mike and the girls during that time were garden-related as they fostered my growing passion. Wide-brimmed hats and special gloves, garden aprons with big pockets, journals, plaques, bunny statues, and other garden art were all welcome in my new world of the *jardin*. I became Garden Gail—at last, my true identity!

Best of all, my newfound, enduring relationship with Mother Nature started to reveal truths and lessons that would serve me well the rest of my life. Patience, sequence of bloom, our temporal lack of control—I found one gem after another to be treasured. I was reminded of a needlepoint canvas created by my mother when I was a child. It proclaimed, "Après la pluie, le beau temps." It hung in our home for years as I queried the unfamiliar words. It translates from French to "After the rain, comes good weather" or literally, "the good times." My family and I had been through rain and storms, and now we were reveling in "le beau temps." The long years in Dallas, the waiting and uncertainty, were all behind us now. This was home, and it tasted like banana pudding on the porch swing.

Our years in Carolina were fulfilling and satisfying. By our ten-year anniversary in the Southern Part of Heaven, the garden had been on three local garden tours, and its reputation was growing. We loved to share the garden with others and fed on the encouraging kind words of guests. "I can just feel the love," was my all-time favorite remark from a visitor, as truly it was an act of love for us to care for this living, growing space. Mike gave me all the credit, but he did the grunt work and was also the chairman of the finance committee. Even though he claimed not to be a gardener, he knew his role was indispensable, and he exhibited an undeniable pride as he saw happy attendees wandering through the paths. It bolstered our desire to keep improving the garden and sharing it with others. During the next ten years, the garden would continue to become well-known, attracting gardening groups on bus tours, becoming the site for various club picnics and other celebrations. We were thrilled to be contacted by local and state magazines for a story and photos, then soon learned a national magazine would be coming for a comprehensive photo shoot. This session resulted in a six-page cover story to be released a year later!

After taking a few years off to "recharge his batteries," Mike applied with FEMA and began a new twelve-year career. His job involved traveling all over the country, the Caribbean, and even Guam, to help manage federal assistance after a disaster. Hurricanes, wildfires, and floods became the center of his new world. He loved the thrill of going to the ROC (regional operating center) when a new storm was brewing and being one of the first responders. He was a comptroller, involved in financial and administrative support for the emergency response teams. My years of flying and travel experience helped me adjust to his new lifestyle to which I could easily relate. What a strange coincidence it was that for the first half of our marriage my job involved traveling, then later he was the one with the suitcase. We supported each other and made it work.

FEMA turned out to be an adventure for us both. With the girls on to their new lives, I was free to visit Mike on deployment, which I greatly enjoyed. Who would not jump at the chance to attend the Iowa State Fair to eat a pork chop on a stick and see the full-size cow made out of butter by the "Butter Lady"? We saw the covered bridges of Madison County made famous by the movie of the same name and wandered through a cornfield at the *Field of Dreams* movie site. On a later trip to New

England, we enjoyed the gorgeous fall leaves and local apple orchards, Ben and Jerry's original ice cream shop, and Norman Rockwell's homeland. A rustic ferry transported us to Martha's Vineyard where I savored my first lobster roll. On beautiful Lake George, we enjoyed lunch on the scenic boat tour. Mike was in San Juan and Florida during the years of multiple hurricanes and had extended stays in both. From San Juan, the most exciting side trip ever was to the Island of Vieques made famous by the shimmering iridescent water at night. While in Orlando after the Florida Four (hurricanes), I visited often, and we sampled the sumptuous restaurants and multiple trips to Disney World. Santa Fe was incredible with its scenery, famous spas, and the Georgia O'Keeffe Museum. One spring, he called me and sang the opening lyrics from the tender Dave Loggins song, "Please Come to Boston"...and I did. He arranged an unforgettable visit to the most incredible lilac park, knowing how I dearly loved lilacs. Well-known Arnold Arboretum was at peak bloom for our arrival, and what a showcase of lilacs it displayed. We got our fill of the freshest seafood imaginable at several of the great Boston hangouts. Conversely, the absolute worst was the Katrina aftermath. Mike spent months there, and when I visited, he took me on a behind-the-scenes tour, with images of devastation I will never be able to wipe from my memory.

During these FEMA years, we also experienced our "decade of weddings." Both daughters found and married their husbands within a six-year period that was marked with much celebration and happiness for our family. Another deeply personal thing occurred during this time between Mike and me, concerning our church attendance. I rarely went to church anymore after the girls left for college, admittedly disliking attending church alone. What had I done all those years ago by going along with the Catholic mandate that he not "interfere" with my raising our children as Catholic? Of course, he always could have joined us by his own volition, but coming from his Southern Baptist upbringing, that proved to be too far a leap. I now could look back and think to myself that I wish I had encouraged him to join me in finding a church where we could *both* feel comfortable and raise our girls there, with both parents attending worship. I wish I had had the courage and foresight, but at that time, I was much too immature to even consider going against church regulations or bucking the system. And where did that leave me? Both girls were raised Catholic as I had promised with my wedding vows, but they were grown now, and how they lived out their future church lives was up to them. My obligation had been fulfilled, and I was left without someone to share church with, leaving me to reap what I had sown.

Mary Evelyn's wedding was held in Georgia near Atlanta in a beautiful old Presbyterian church, which she and Andy had been attending. Andy had been raised in that faith, and it felt comfortable to Mary Evelyn. It was a good match. Mike and I loved the minister and everything about how the church staff conducted the wedding events over the few days. It was the most time he had spent in a church in decades. I could tell he liked it. After the wedding, he was back on deployment with FEMA, and I was back home with a new idea. Maybe I should check out our local Presbyterian church and see how it compared to the one in Georgia. Maybe, what if...?

I went to University Presbyterian Church every Sunday he was gone to get a feel for it. I loved it! I loved the sanctuary, the music, the ministers, the sermons, and the friendly people, many of whom I already knew as members of my small-town community. This was it—yes, it might work. I got my nerve up and broached this taboo subject about which we never spoke. I really did not know what kind of reaction to expect, but I decided it was worth the try. I composed a long e-mail explaining my proposition and my reasons, whispered a prayer, and sent it off to him. I told him about the local church and how much I liked it. I asked him to consider going there with me for three months, whenever he was in town, and if at the end of the time he did not want to continue, I would let it drop. He replied within moments, "Okay."

I was nervous the first time we attended together, but it went great, and he was hooked. We never even talked about the three months again. He loved it as much as I did—maybe more. I could tell he was just starved for this, and I felt so badly that circumstances existed to keep him away from church with his family all these years. He loved meeting and getting to know all the ministers, making the sermons so much more personal. Within a few months, we heard Pastor Bob announce this routine invitation, "If you are interested in church membership, please speak to one of the staff."

I looked at Mike and said, "I think he was talking to you." We signed up for New Member Sunday, and the rest is history. We officially joined the church together a few weeks later, and there were no words for my joy.

A few years later, our daughter Amy became engaged, and the wedding would be held at our church. It was a dream wedding with all the trimmings, highlighted by Mike proudly walking the beautiful bride down the center aisle of the church we both so loved.

Months later as we drove home from early service, we were discussing the sermon as we often did when he paused, shook his head slightly left and right, and said, "I love that little church," and I swear there was a tear in his eye. I was flooded with regret as I thought about the circumstances that prevented our family from attending the same church and worshiping together all those years. I knew my part in it, and that hurt most of all. *What had I done?*

Our lives continued to unfold as lives do. Our beautiful daughters provided us with birthdays, graduations, weddings, and babies as our family grew in size and love. Mary Evelyn and Andy gave us our first grand-child in 2006, a precious baby girl named Ella Kathryn. She was our joy, and we saw her as often as possible. Mike was perhaps her greatest admirer and loved to walk her in the stroller, sit with her by the high chair as she nibbled Cheerios, and push her on the baby swing in the garden. A couple of years later, we welcomed a boy they named Norwood, our family name, who would be called Woody for short. Soon after Amy and Don married, we were blessed with our second grandson, Sam, whose middle name was Michael after his papa. Mike embraced his new role and adored all his grandchildren, as they adored him right back. Our family was the center of our lives, and we were so grateful for them every day—every short day and every long day. As for me, fond sentiments of my days as a young mother still resonated, perhaps even more strongly now. Gretchen Rubin captured such a kernel of truth when she wrote, "The days are long, but the years are short." So true for a new mother and truer still for a new grandmother.

4

Detour to Hell

When you came, you were
like red wine and honey
And the taste of you burnt
my mouth with its sweetness.
Now you are like morning
bread, smooth and pleasant.
I hardly taste you at all
for I know your savor,
But I am completely
nourished.

—"Decade" by Amy Lowell

*M*ike retired from FEMA in 2010 so we could spend more time with our growing family. In 2012, we happily celebrated our fortieth wedding anniversary at our home with close friends and family. Well aware that was not traditional, we had been hearing about other couples opting to celebrate before the fiftieth. We had no idea at that time what a blessing it would be that we did not wait. I wrote a toast to deliver during our anniversary dinner, ending with these verses:

Now forty years later we are still a pair
With a few more pounds
and a little less hair.
Our greatest joy then and
our greatest joy now
Are our two little girls who showed us how
To be a family with ups and downs
To love—to grow—to turn around.

Now they are married, our family grows
Adding two fine men we are proud to know.
We are blessed with three grands
and one on the way;
His name is Papa and I am Mémé.

So here's to family, and here's to friends
Here's to a love that never ends.
Here's to you and here's to me,
Happy Anniversary!

This celebration prompted both Mike and me to focus on and appreciate our love, our marriage, and our lives together. We had made it through so much—our careers, our little girls growing into strong, impressive young women, some frightening health issues, and the four-year interruption of our togetherness, as we transitioned from Dallas to Chapel Hill. Evenings would find us on the covered back deck, sipping wine and listening to country music. I would be nestled into pillows on the porch swing while Mike sat rhythmically back-and-forthing in his cushioned glider.

When George Jones sang his hit song "He Stopped Loving Her Today," Mike asked me if I knew what those words meant. I nodded, but he continued, "He stopped loving her the day he died, and not before." He paused, then looked at me, and said, "That's how it is with you and me." Then he sweetly told me, as he had many times, "You know you're the love of my life and always have been." Then and there, I savored again the morning bread, smooth and pleasant. Not overly romantic on a regular basis, I treasured this rare intimate exchange. Mike always came through. Even though our marriage had grown into a typical mature relationship with the usual warts and freckles, in the end, I was his and he was mine. We had each other. Our complete love, devotion, and loyalty was rock solid, could not be denied, and for that, I would be forever grateful.

Our fourth grandchild was born the following February. Another little boy, Isaac, was welcomed with open arms. Life was good. With family around us, we comfortably settled into this new chapter as retirees and grandparents. We were both healthy, in our sixties, and our work lives were finished. Our focus now was our family and our established home and garden, where we hoped to stay for many more years. A bonus was being able to attend church together regularly now that he was retired, something we both loved dearly. While many retirees opt for travel in these golden years, it was not high on our bucket list. We had both traveled often for work, and for us, being home was quite the treat. The girls and their families were strong and growing, and we cherished being with our young grandchildren. We had so much going for us, so much to be thankful for, and so much to look forward to. But as it turns out, we were enjoying a false sense of well-being, having no idea what would soon befall us.

In September, with great anticipation, we attended a Norwood family wedding. Our nephew and godson Patrick was getting married in New Orleans, with its distinct French and Spanish architecture, Creole cuisine, and vibrant nightlife. Jazz filled the air in this perfect setting, and the riverfront bustled with the essence of the Crescent City. The Catholic wedding ceremony was held in the magnificent St. Louis Cathedral, and Mike and I had a small role as his godparents. The mood was very celebratory, and we were especially grateful to be able to see so many of Mike's siblings and extended family members. If we could only freeze this delicious little slice of life we were tasting right now!

A couple of weeks after returning home, it started. Mike did not feel well. He stated somberly, "I don't know, something's just not right." Shortly thereafter, we attended the baptism of our new grandson, but Mike had to excuse himself from the church. It hit so fast. When we got home, he could not eat, and he slept practically around-the-clock. The doctor suspected some food poisoning he might have picked up on the trip. His blood pressure was low. They adjusted his meds and scheduled another checkup in a few days as needed.

Our forty-first wedding anniversary came and went that same week. I dutifully picked up a card and handed it to him as he sat pale and still in his favorite chair. Thoughts of our glorious anniversary celebration a year ago flooded my mind with gratitude. We had already started talking about what we might do for our fiftieth, never imagining we might not make it that far.

Within a few days, he became so weak he could not even walk on his own. I would help him limp from one place to the next as needed. I was terribly disturbed at his rapid decline, his lack of appetite, and apparent confusion. Suddenly, he could not figure out how to operate the TV remote control, which had previously been second nature to him. Something was very wrong. He shunned going back to the doctor, saying he just needed more time. I look back now with a heavy heart and realize I should have insisted, but at that moment, I had no idea it was so serious; it was common for Mike to resist medical attention. I was confused and distressed by his condition, had not ever seen symptoms like this before, and I just did not know what to do.

When we woke on Saturday morning, his condition was alarmingly worse, and I knew we could not wait any longer. His eyes foretold an impending crisis. His skin color was off. His weak state was disconcerting. As usual, he objected to the idea of seeing a doctor, preferring to wait until Monday, but I threatened that either he let me help him to the car and drive him to the ER, or I was going to call an ambulance. He became anxious and vehemently opposed a trip to the ER, so we compromised on a nearby Urgent Care Center.

I texted our girls quickly to let them know we were going for help. I managed to get some clothes on him and carefully supported him as we headed to the car. His dense weight on my smaller frame was unsteady and inauspicious as he leaned on me. I was terrified about descending the four brick steps off the front porch. His right hand clinched the handrail, and his left arm was slung over my back and shoulder. He was so heavy, and one step after the other, I feared we would both topple over with the slightest miscalculation. We survived the descent and inched around the car to the passenger seat where I helped him with his seat belt. As we pulled out of the driveway, he turned to me with a look in his eyes I had never seen before and mumbled, "There is something bad wrong with me."

I got a wheelchair from the lobby of Urgent Care, carefully transferred him into it, and pushed him inside. I had never seen my big, strong man in a wheelchair before, and something about that image went through me like a bolt of lightning. Where did his big and strong go? What was happening? Fear was overtaking us both as we acknowledged a huge unknown. We got admitted to an examination room, and the doctor came quickly. She addressed Mike, asking what had been going on, and even in his weakened state, he started sugarcoating the developments of the past week. I had to interrupt and ask him to allow me to relay a more factual account. The doctor ordered an echocardiogram, and he was now stretched out on the table, his labored breathing more evident than before. When the doctor returned with the test results, she said immediately, "Mr. Norwood, you belong in the hospital. You may have a pulmonary embolism, but whatever it is, we cannot treat you here. Would you like your wife to drive you to the ER or shall I call an ambulance?"

Preliminary tests after just a few hours revealed pneumonia. This sounded hopeful. It took until almost midnight for a bed to open up in the ICU, then more testing. Shock replaced the earlier glimpse of promise as we learned he not only had pneumonia but in fact had contracted Legionnaires' disease, a severe form of pneumonia. I joined the girls in a conference call about 1:00 a.m. as the nurses settled him into his room. With an aching heart, I told my daughters the recent news. The reality of the moment catapulted us into a greater dimension of fear than we had ever known. Before we said good night at that late hour, we tenderly recited the words of the Lord's Prayer together, with more passion and urgency than we had ever done before. Painfully aware of the seriousness of the situation, we begged God to spare his life and return him to our loving care.

The doctors felt sure he picked something up on the wedding trip to New Orleans a little over two weeks before. Most of the family had rooms in a quaint, charming hotel right in the French Quarter. Decorative black wrought iron tables and chairs filled a large courtyard in the middle of the four brick walls. A huge fountain in the center was the focal point. The splashes and sprays of misting water dancing out in every direction would have been a perfect vehicle for the transmission of the waterborne bacteria called Legionella, which causes the illness commonly known as Legionnaires' disease. No one else in our party got sick. The CDC was soon in touch with me to add details of Mike's diagnosis to national tracking statistics, report it to our hotel in New Orleans, and inform the Louisiana Department of Health. While the bacteria often strikes several people who are commonly exposed, we were told random solitary cases do occur.

During the first week in ICU, he showed some improvement. Targeted antibiotics were administered along with other fluids to counteract his recent decline. The staff seemed confident they could get this under control. He was smiling and eating, and we were busily planning how to get him out of there as quickly as possible. Thanksgiving was just a few weeks away, and we had previously made plans to be in the mountains with both the girls' families and our grandkids for the holiday. We had put a deposit down on a fantastic VRBO for the ten of us, with breathtaking views from the deck, three king-size beds, a gourmet kitchen, and plenty of room for all four little ones. He told me he did not want to lose the house and instructed me to send in the remaining rental fee. We were so encouraged and relieved—we had dodged the bullet.

But as each day wore on, our hope diminished. Just as quickly as he had improved the first week, he declined in the second. He gradually ceased to respond to the treatments. We were asked if we would agree to the use of a ventilator for Mike if the need arose. The nurses explained it was best for the family to consider the option and make the decision before some critical moment when it may be difficult to think straight. As with everything, there were pros and cons. But yes, we all agreed that if a ventilator was needed for his survival, then of course, *yes*! Soon afterward, he suffered a severe downward turn. He was abruptly intubated. The tube was in, down his larynx, forcing air into his lungs as he was no longer able to do on his own. The precious breath of life was being provided by this miraculous machine until his body could catch up and begin to heal.

Mary Evelyn came from Georgia, and she and Amy were with me in the hospital as much as they could possibly be. Even during this time of intubation when he was not conscious, their visits were frequent and loving. They sat by their dad and kept a cool cloth on his brow, something we knew he enjoyed. They read to him, talked to him, and held his limp hand. We staggered our visits and rotated in and out so one of us was with him most of each and every day. On occasion when I was with him alone, I would stand by his bed and take his hand in mine. I would look in disbelief at his frail body tethered by endless tubes and wires, with the ventilator mask secured to his face, helping him breathe. Through tears, I begged him, "Please don't leave me, please, please don't leave me!" There was no response. *Could he even hear me?* I asked him to squeeze my hand, but nothing. Oh, how I wished he could have squeezed back! Days passed, and his condition became more and more dire.

During these tender weeks, we were lifted up by visits from our three pastors, Bob, John, and Anna. Mike loved the sermons of our Senior Pastor Bob and was touched by his frequent attention. John was younger and oversaw the active Campus Ministry at church, an organization for which Mike served as treasurer, so he and John were well acquainted. Anna was primarily responsible for the hospital pastoral visits where her giving and outgoing personality made her perfectly suited for this challenging task. Near the age of our daughters, we counted on her for a supply of uplifting scripture and her unfailing support.

One day when Anna was there with us in the ICU, we were all asked to leave the room for about an hour while the doctors inserted a new central line catheter in Mike's chest. There in the waiting room down the hall the conversation turned to Anna and her pastoral work.

I asked, "Anna, how can you bear to do this all the time, to visit families and be around so much illness and death? How do you keep coming back?" The answer came quickly, as if she had been asked before.

"It's so rich," she replied with surety. She commented more to clarify, but to me, that word made no sense; it did not fit. I found her remark unexpected and curious. What did she mean by *so rich*? Those words to me imply something of value, something of abundance, something positive. I understood she was seeing it from a different point of view, but I could see or feel nothing *rich* about what we were living out with each throbbing day. On the contrary, I felt uniquely poor and robbed. I did not have the strength to give it any more thought, and I dismissed the conversation from my mind.

One dreary November day when I was alone with Mike in the ICU, the attending doctor entered and asked me bluntly how long I was going to "keep my loved one on life support?" A feeling of betrayal washed over me at the suggestion that this therapeutic intubation recommended by the medical staff had morphed into life support and that I was somehow now responsible for prolonging it. My heart sank, and the shreds of hope I had so desperately held on to pulled away from me and spun into nothingness.

The ugly reality fell crashing down on all of us. Doctors told us his lungs had deteriorated so greatly that he would never breathe on his own again, never walk on his own again, and that he would never come home again. At best, he would bounce around between rehab facilities and hospitals, constantly on oxygen, and bound to a wheelchair for the rest of his life. We knew he would not want that. He was not going to make it, and we were frozen at the realization. We prayed for strength to cope. Pastor Anna came to be with me, and in my tearful state of shock, I asked her, "Is this the valley of the shadow of death?"

She nodded yes, took my hand, then said, "But we walk *through* it."

I could not believe that this man of mine with whom I had spent my entire adult life was about to leave me forever after only a few short weeks of illness. Were we not just joyfully dancing and celebrating with family at our godson's wedding? Were we not just marching through the streets of the French Quarter with the wedding party's Second Line parade, waving our *fleur-de-lis* handkerchiefs? Were we not just fishing with our grandkids in a nearby pond while they visited on fall break just days before his hospitalization? Were we not just sitting on the back deck, just the two of us sipping a glass of wine, and listening to country music as evening fell? And damn that mountain retreat getaway! Only brief weeks earlier, we were excitedly planning details of meals and events for this special holiday adventure, and now it scornfully mocked us. We could not have imagined in our wildest dreams that instead of delighting in special family time together for Thanksgiving, we would be preparing to say goodbye to him forever.

I dug out his medical directive in which he clearly stated he did not wish to be kept alive on life support. That meant extubation; the doctors advised us how to proceed. We were told that once the tubing to the ventilator was removed, Mike may stop breathing in ten minutes or ten days. He might regain consciousness, and he might not. Therefore, they would not proceed with this step until Mary Evelyn and her family arrived from Georgia on Monday. Even though Amy and her family lived nearby, they would also stay in Chapel Hill so we could all be together. There was plenty of room upstairs in their old bedrooms, and this way, we could hold each other up. It was such a blessing to have the house full of the people closest to me especially our dear grandchildren, along with baby Isaac who always made us smile.

We could almost feel the angels hovering. Mary Evelyn's family arrived on Monday, and the doctors scheduled the detachment from his ventilator for Tuesday. Time was up. We had to face the fact that these would be his final days and our final days together. We waited nearby while the respiratory therapists delicately worked that hard, once life-giving tube out and up through his weary throat. We held our breath. He survived the procedure, and we quickly returned to his side. He had lost significant weight, and it hurt to see him so compromised. Those big, strong arms that used to hold us all tight had all but shriveled away. He did gain consciousness briefly giving us a chance to see his beautiful blue eyes again. We could, and we did, shower him with our love for those precious minutes. He could not speak, and his mouth was frozen open after weeks of having that unmalleable tube down his throat. It was a gift to see him awake again after weeks of being completely unresponsive. But the bigger gift was at least a little time for us to all gather so we could be present for him and for each other in his final moments.

The girls made arrangements with the ICU nurses that should an emergency or the end come during the night, they would call one of them, instead of me, to spare me that burden. We knew it would be very soon. Just a couple of days after the extubation, Amy came into my bedroom in early dawn and gently wakened me.

"Mom, we have to go quickly, the nurse just called."

Without even pausing to feel the fear, we threw on our clothes and were in the car in minutes. It was still dark, and the cold winter air was piercing. We drove there in silence, parked illegally, and ran up to the room. Several nurses and respiratory therapists were gathered around him, shouting, "Michael, keep breathing! Stay with us! Breathe!" They were keeping him alive for us, until we arrived.

When we entered and rushed to him, they all left except Adrienne, a nurse we knew well, who had cared for him many days. She turned the hanging monitor showing his heart rate and vitals away from us so we could not see it. Then she left us alone with him. We stood by his bed sobbing, holding his hands and each other's, praying for him, telling him we loved him, and thanking God for his life.

I opened my phone to a message from Pastor Bob who had sent me a prayer for the end, should we need it. At Mike's bedside with my two precious girls on either side of me, I tearfully offered up the poignant words of this old Anglican commendation:

> Michael, our companion in faith and our brother in Christ, we entrust you now to God.
>
> Go forth in the love of the Father who created you, the mercy of Jesus Christ who died for you, and the power of the Holy Spirit, who accompanies you.

At one with all the faithful, living and departed, may you rest in peace and rise in glory, where grief and misery are banished, and light and joy evermore abide. Amen.

A stillness fell. Adrienne reentered, and I looked at her. My eyes asked what I could not put into words. She nodded, and I was touched by the genuinely sorrowful look on her face. "He has passed," she said softly. I looked up to the ceiling as if to watch him ascend with the angels who had come to claim him.

In my heart, I echoed the words, "Rest in peace and rise in glory, my love." I blew him a kiss and whispered goodbye.

That was the day before Thanksgiving 2013. It had been forty days and forty nights in the ICU. Forty days and forty nights that Jesus fasted and prayed in the desert. Forty days and forty nights in Lent that invite us to join Him in that sacred time of preparation. Forty days and forty nights between the resurrection of Jesus on that first Easter day until His ascension into heaven. Forty days and forty nights that the rains fell in the great flood. *Forty sacred days and forty sacred nights.* Forty days and forty nights that our family had been paralyzed with fear and dread as our dear husband, father, and grandfather slipped away from us.

Once home, I had to take care of some business but felt strangely suspended in the moment. It was as if my sudden lack of direction collided with the present urgency, and the two broke into an ugly brawl. But the brawl was in my head and my heart, forcing its way down into my stomach full of knots. Mike was gone, time stood still, and life as I knew it was over. I was not even sure what any of that meant in terms of reality. I only had a numbing premonition that it was bad—very, very bad.

I was obligated to notify family, our pastors, the morgue, and the funeral home. Those calls were torturous, attempting to verbalize what had happened and hearing the condolences offered in return. His four siblings were devastated but would notify extended family and make plans to attend the service. We would come together to hold each other up and share this dreadful, unexpected loss.

Looking back now, I do not even know how I got through that day. I felt so detached, so robotic. My girls and their husbands did the last-minute shopping, and they all worked in the kitchen to prep for the impending Thanksgiving dinner. What a comfort it was to have all of them there with me, and it was so touching to see how the older grandchildren expressed sadness that their papa was gone. My seven-year-old granddaughter helped me set the table and fold the turkey napkins we had used for years. She blessed me with a long, sweet hug as we tried to comfort each other. We arranged the chairs, and I felt a deep pang at needing one fewer this year.

When the time arrived the next day for the feast, I sat at my usual end of the table, and we left the space empty at the opposite end, where Mike should have been sitting, offering the holiday prayer of thanks and carving the turkey. I had written a few words to say for grace, to somehow try to capture a genuine sense of gratitude in spite of the penetrating loss we were all feeling. Don and Andy had both lost their fathers in recent years, one to MS and one to dementia. It was recent enough to be palpable, and Mike's death served as a painful reminder. We were gathered in communal lament. All three of these beloved fathers were sorely missed, and we closed by thanking our heavenly Father for the gift of them all in our lives.

The autumn holiday had loomed wide and deep through much of this. When Mike's demise came on the very eve of Thanksgiving, we could not help but shift our focus from the pain and shock of losing him to joyful gratitude. One of the hymns in his memorial service was chosen for these special words:

> Let all things now living—a
> song of thanksgiving
> To God the creator trium-
> phantly raise.
> Who fashioned and made us,
> protected and stayed us,
> Who still guides us on to the
> end of our days.

One may wonder which is best: the long goodbye or the short goodbye? Most probably, it is desirable that we do not get to choose the timing of the end for ourselves or our loved ones. Each is uniquely insidious and benevolent. Their visceral nature renders comparison impossible. There are surely blessings and curses with each, creating yet another mystery in our lives, another mystery to embrace, because we are at a loss for how else to respond. In faith, we are called to embrace many mysteries—of the past and the future, of love and fear, and the great mystery of death and rebirth, loss and renewal. We long for the fullness of life, but instead, we may get an unfinished song. Try as we do to hold on to the melody, it keeps fading. We even forget the lyrics in time. And it hurts so much to miss the finale we have been joyfully anticipating. We have known an end, but it was not the end we wanted. We may pray for the peace of God, the peace that transcends all understanding. And we acknowledge there are just some things on this side of *heaven* we will never be able to fully comprehend.

> *My ticket to the dark*
> *side just arrived.*
> *It is one way, and*
> *nonreturnable.*
> *I'll be leaving soon.*

5

The Dream

If it be thus to dream,
Still let me sleep.

—William Shakespeare

The end of the third year after Mike died led into yet another difficult holiday season. But this year, for the first time, I put up some decorations. No tree, just a few touches here and there, a wreath on the door, and some candles. I was starting to feel a little brighter. The new year began as did my fourth year as a widow. Thoughts about my future crept in. *Should I stay in the house or think about a move?* A few friends asked if I had considered dating, and I only briefly let that possibility tiptoe into my thoughts. I could not imagine how it would be to date again after all these years.

As the fourth spring approached, I sensed a turning point. I was all cried out and plain weary of feeling so low. An irritability crept over me when I saw in my shadow this cranky, lonely widow. *Who was this stranger?* I wanted to shake off that false persona and kick it to the curb. That is not me! I started to think about choices. What are my choices? Do I even have a choice?

Just asking myself that small question opened a place in my heart where I could at last begin to process my experiences and use them to move forward. It was a sort of threshold, and in just that simple act of wondering about a new future, I stepped over from one mental platform to another. I suffered over three terrible years, pushing me to the very brink of what I could endure. The resounding loneliness, the isolation, the tears and depression, the brush with breast cancer, the debilitating hip and knee pain persisting over two years, and the neglect of my beloved garden were all dreadful reminders of my time in *grief prison*. I wanted out from behind these bars. Perhaps my parole would finally come through. My college friend Kathy, who had long ago lost an adult son and had suffered terribly with her grief, wrote me these encouraging words, which she had found inspiring: "First we survive, then we endure, then we fully live again." I had survived, and I had endured. But will I ever fully live again? It was time I gave myself permission to rejoin the living.

I looked at my life and took a thorough inventory. I loved my house and garden, but being alone here just was not the same as sharing it with someone. Much of my daily activity revolved around keeping them both up, but at the end of the day, I had to ask myself why. Doing it only for me and the occasional visit from my grandkids did not seem to make sense anymore. Eating alone and being alone were shining a glaring light at my new reality. As grateful as I was for my many blessings, something was missing. I had heard that in order to get what I wanted, I needed to truly understand what that was. I had to get clear and ask myself these hard questions. What choices did I have? Could I truly choose to be happy again? Could I choose to fill the empty parts of my heart by opening up to possibilities again?

Maybe instead of pulling weeds, I could choose to go out to lunch with an interesting man. Maybe if one thing led to another, perhaps I could rediscover the simple joy of holding hands again after all these years. I did not know what I truly wanted, and I had only started wondering. A few encouraging nudges from friends kept it on my mind. Was it time? I was reluctant to step into murky waters with which I was so unacquainted, but I knew other people did it with some success. For months, I examined my life and prayed to become clear about what I wanted. I realized we are all worthy of happiness, but I wondered if I was ready to share my life again? I asked my daughters for their blessings, and they reluctantly acquiesced. I am not sure they were fully aware of how difficult things had been for me, as I always put on a happy face for them so they would not worry. But somehow, they read between the lines and

offered their support. I felt cautiously optimistic, seasoned with a pinch of curiosity.

Dating had changed quite a bit over the
years, and my foray into the online scene was
fraught with anxiety. I had a friend help me
get set up, and I began. I prepared for my new
adventure with a look at my wardrobe, which
had been sadly neglected. As I shopped for
new apparel, I thought back on recent years
when I was stuck in my version of prison garb
for so long. Dark clothes with no jewelry and
little makeup—that was behind me now. I
tried on some earrings. It felt good. A certain
bracelet matched my skirt. It stayed. Baby
steps… I was waking up. *Deep breaths.*

Learning how things worked in this
world of online dating was a challenge, and
I struggled to find my place. I had to kiss a
few frogs, but I was getting my feet wet. In
October, my high school class hosted our fiftieth anniversary reunion, a festive celebration of dear lifelong friends in Williamsburg.
Being with many of the guys from my youth

and sharing such a good time with everyone only encouraged me. I realized that I genuinely *liked* having a conversation and connection with these men I had known as boys. I had no idea what was ahead, but I felt myself opening up to the possibilities of a new day, and perhaps a new life.

Before I knew it, the holidays were upon us, and I took a break from the dating sites. The New Year rang in, with typical rhetoric about setting goals, a fresh start, and new beginnings, which spoke to me as never before. I considered the possibility of putting the house on the market and significantly changing my lifestyle. For almost twenty-seven years, this had been my home, and I really did not want to leave. I truly loved the neighborhood, my dream house, and the special garden we had built around it, prompting me to seriously question if it would be in my best interest to sell or not. There was no clear answer, but maybe caring for this grand abode and garden was something I should release. In my own mind, it was questionable, but my daughters and my realtor-sister thought it was a great idea and encouraged me, adding they thought it was way past due.

With my doubts and a leap of faith, I moved forward. January and February were consumed with interviewing realtors and getting the house staged and decluttered for showing. It went live in early March just in time for the spring season to showcase the garden, a feature the realtor was highly promoting. Early spring treasures punctuated the landscape with bursts of color: the bluish-purple grape hyacinths, the pink fuchsia, and yellow crocuses, and the brilliant blue Siberian scillas. The early blooming eight-foot-tall pearlbush was in its glory, adding a brilliant white accent to a quiet corner. The paths and beds were tidied and primed, and the house never looked better. No doubt some serious decluttering of my soul was also taking place. I considered the many advantages of a fresh start and hoped I was doing the right thing.

After the real estate launch in early March, I got back into the online dating. My plan was to sell the house and to be open to any future developments in my personal life. I felt much more prepared and confident about a new relationship than I did back in late September. I signed up for a couple of dating sites, then stood back to see what might happen. I was encouraged by the response and enjoyed this new feeling of anticipation. The attention and flirting felt good.

One man in particular caught my eye, but something bothered me. His profile name was Port McMichael, so I guessed his name was *Michael*. I just could not go there. *Another Mike?* He had a lot of facial hair—not my style. I did not reply. He was persistent, so I reconsidered. I liked his profile, and he was quite handsome in spite of the beard. I answered him, and my first question was "Do you go by Mike or Michael?" He immediately replied *Michael*, which he considered more professional for his work as a psychiatric nurse practitioner. The next day, he wanted to switch to texting, which was easier. We texted back and forth, and the conversation had begun.

The next morning, I received a photo he had taken on his way to work, saying, "Thinking of you and wondering when I saw this sunrise, if this is the dawn of something more than just a new day?"

When he got home from work later, we started hours of long texts back and forth. We shared a French heritage of which we were both proud. I spoke of my Parisian mother, and he was French Canadian. "Could we talk on the phone?" he asked. It was wonderful! So much in common and the conversation, so easy. He asked if he could take me to lunch on Saturday—he would come to Chapel Hill from Greensboro, and I would choose the restaurant.

From the very start, it was like a dream, a dream come true. Our first date was on St. Patrick's Day, and we joked about it being our lucky day even though we were not Irish. Maybe we would find a rainbow and a pot of gold. I tried to control my jitters. A little French restaurant for our first date seemed appropriate. When I drove up, he was waiting out front, and I recognized him immediately. His big, beautiful smile was contagious, and he waved when he saw me. It was instant attraction, smooth and natural.

He was delightfully charming and entertaining, and the mood was divine. Two long, pleasant hours passed, and neither of us wanted it to end. As we approached the parking lot after lunch, we decided to prolong our visit with a walk. We found a perfect trail with benches near a creek. A beautiful spring day reflected our mood of new beginnings. As we sat and talked, details of his life just poured out. "I don't know why I'm telling you all this," he would say, "I just want you to know." His wife of nearly thirty years and mother of his children had died just over nine years prior of esophageal cancer. He was a prostate cancer survivor of over sixteen years and doing well. I told him about my brush with breast cancer, then shared more of my personal history.

We sat there on the park bench, arm in arm, and so content. The sun was dipping as we walked back to the car.

"I'd like to see you again," he said, and I nodded in agreement. He asked when, and I fumbled for a moment.

Then I bravely suggested, "How about tomorrow?" A bright smile came over his face, and I knew I had said the right thing.

Our first tomorrow came, and I met him in Greensboro so he could take me to his favorite Chinese restaurant, then show me his condo. Afterward we went to a park where we slowly walked hand in hand and lingered on a low brick wall, drinking in another glorious spring day. Before we left, he showed me the memorial brick for his late wife, which was one of many in the meandering park path. Sharing something so personal with me at this early moment was surprising. But he repeated what he had said the day before, that he wanted me to know everything about his life, and he was not sure why. I was touched by his honestly, and it opened the door to what would become a deep intimacy between us.

Next, we stopped by his condo for a tour and a short visit. The coffee table was covered with travel brochures, mostly Mediterranean cruises. He had been dreaming about making this trip a reality and casually suggested what fun it would be for us to go together. Astonished at how right it felt so soon, we knew this was a beautiful beginning. The attraction was undeniable. Before I left for home, he asked if we could meet halfway for dinner in a few days? And so it began.

It was like stepping out of my black-and-white world of the past four years into a technicolor movie scene. I felt awake and alive. The next few weeks flew by in a flurry of wonder and romance. He wanted to see me as often as possible, and I was flattered at his endearing attention.

Within the first month, we got two rooms and spent a long weekend at the beach, not heeding my daughters' caution that it was "entirely too soon for that." But it did not feel too soon—it felt perfect. We lingered over coffee and muffins looking out at the ocean from our hotel deck. Later we enjoyed a slow walk along the beach, exhilarating in the warm sand under our bare feet and the spring wind in our hair. We took selfie after selfie, seeing in them this happy new couple, that was *us*. We were falling in love.

We continued to thrive and flourish. He drove my sister and me to a family reunion in the mountains of Pennsylvania and bravely subjected himself for a few days to fifty strangers who were protective of me. They loved him right away as I knew they would. One of my cousins told us very seriously that this love we shared was unmistakable and rare and that we best hold on to it with all our might. Deep down, we knew he was right.

I was happy to meet his daughter, Niki, and her fiancé, Zac, early on for dinner, and they were most welcoming. Their wedding was just a few weeks away, and Michael had said to me, "You *will* accompany me to my daughter's wedding!" I resisted, knowing how hard it would be for Niki not to have her mama there on that special day. But Niki was most gracious and made me feel comfortable, insisting that I attend.

As we left the restaurant, she said to me privately, "I don't know if I should say this, but my papa is the best father and the best husband in the world, and he deserves the very best." I hoped I could be that—for her and for him.

The dream continued. A medical conference in New York City was coming up, and he invited me to join him. We saw three Broadway shows in four days including *Phantom of the Opera*, which I had never seen. We ate well, hopping around from picturesque pubs to restaurants like Carmine's, and we did not miss the opportunity to indulge in a Reuben and a beer at an authentic neighborhood deli. One night after a show, he hailed a pedicab, and we rode New York-style through all the glitz and glory of Time Square back to our hotel. Such *joie de vivre!* We were both awake again. We were alive again!

The house was still on the market with ample showings but no offers. We enjoyed our time there, cooking out and eating on the deck, tending the garden, relaxing on the hammock, and just being there together. He was growing comfortable in this setting, and he sensed I did not really want to leave. One day we were getting a sandwich nearby to kill time during a showing, and he shocked me by suggesting we stay in the house—at least for now—until we see where all this is going. This idea was totally unexpected as were the tears that spoke my response. We could not wait to get the For Sale sign out of the front yard and breathe a sigh of relief.

I was back! Up went my best summer wreath on the front door, and colorful flowers filled the footed urns nearby. The American flag went out on Memorial Day and Fourth of July for the first time in years. The deck and terraced patio out back were again adorned with decorative pillows that had gone unused for so long. I cleaned my bluebird boxes, set them out, and happily awaited the arrival of my neglected feathered friends. How I had missed them! Until that moment, I did not really know how much.

With the house issue resolved for now, we eased into a comfortable routine. He was working full time, and we tried to be together as much as possible. We were the same age, both born in 1949 just four months apart. For his sixty-ninth birthday, we went to the beach again to celebrate. I gave him a father of the bride visor and a simple silver cross that he wore around his neck and never took off. In Greensboro for a midweek visit, I met his son, Scott, at dinner out along with Niki and Zac. Their wedding was approaching, and I helped Michael write his toast. The nuptials were breathtaking on the backdrop of a North Carolina mountain resort with a river dancing by. I felt privileged to be at his side for that proud moment in a father's life.

My friends were eager to meet this man who had turned my world upside down. Peggy, Brenda, and Ginger from my early "stewardess" a.k.a. flight attendant days were still dear friends, and we cooked up a visit here at the house. Sadly, Mary Beth had recently passed away from breast cancer, which made us more dedicated than ever to stay in touch. At the last minute, Peggy had to cancel, but the other two came and brought their men. Ginger's Bob was also from Canada and had played pro hockey, so he and Michael immediately hit it off. We all bonded, and they remarked that it seemed we had been together forever, so natural, at ease, and lighting the place up!

A summer trip to Las Vegas was planned complete with tickets to see Celine Dion. Michael hatched the idea, called me, and demanded, "Give me one good reason we should not book it?" I could not think of one! Our room at Caesar's Palace was luxurious with an incredible view and a phenomenal light show out our window every night. We spent hours poolside, enjoying the scenery with Roman columns and statues, alive with impressive fountains, and our first-time swimming together. One evening after a romantic dinner at Bouchon, we floated through the canals of the Venetian Hotel, serenaded by the costumed gondoliers. It was so romantic, and we were the perfect couple to squeeze every bit of fantasy out of it!

With our common interest in all things French, we were eager to check out the Paris Hotel and ooh la la, we immediately loved it! Oozing with quaint European charm, it successfully recreated the feel of the City of Lights, complete with its fifty-story replica of the Eiffel Tower. With our shared love of

Paris, we quickly admitted we would love to go there together some time. The hour-long wait for an oh-so-French lunch at the hotel's bistro *Mon Ami Gabi* was time well spent. Our table was under an awning like a sidewalk café, and we were entertained by passersby, just like in Paris. For starters, we enjoyed traditional French mimosas, chilled champagne mixed with Chambord and adorned with fresh juicy raspberries. *Santè!* We savored incredible French baguettes with soft, sweet cream butter, pâtè, warm brie, and saucisson, followed by authentic steak frites. The fantasy and indulgence of Vegas amazed us with delight and fed our desire to live life to its fullest. And most of all, to live that exciting life with each other.

Back home in Chapel Hill, we continued making life as exciting as possible with each passing day. We became friendly with two local couples, both of whom I had known over twenty years. They were taken in with Michael's friendly personality, but I know that more than that, they were glad he happened along and helped me come alive again. Barbara and Stephen, also American Airlines retirees, lived nearby in Southern Pines and to my delight, immediately befriended my new love. Sharon and David lived in Chapel Hill but were staying in Paris half the year, living out their dream. When they invited us to visit any time and stay in the extra bedroom in their Paris flat, we quickly expressed our interest and gratitude. We would definitely plan on that, perhaps in the fall. It felt so good to share lunches and dinners with these friends and others as we expanded our new social life. To see them react so positively to Michael and to us as a couple only confirmed what we knew deep inside. Over and over, friends of old and even people we did not know very well remarked that our love was palpable and that we even looked different with a new glow on our faces. David remarked, "Gail, I've never seen you like this!"

I was totally captivated by Michael's romantic ways. Early on, he apologized to me for being so corny, but I stopped him and declared myself to be the queen of corn, thus a perfect match. I could take all the corniness he could throw at me. We would welcome each other's sweet nothings with no fear of rejection. We are not writing a new chapter in our lives, he would declare, but a whole new book. A book on second chances, a book on starting over, a book on new life. It would be about emerging from painful loss and being open to fresh possibilities. The main characters were weary and spent, but deep down, all they longed for was to feel the thrill again, to taste the kiss again, and to savor one more chance at life.

Michael spoiled me with our morning ritual of coffee and a sweet treat on a tray in bed as we lingered there, planning our day, and listening to our favorite songs. Our daily gratitude moment always included how thankful we were for hitting the jackpot of love and life. Each day truly was a joy as we discovered how seamlessly our lives had come together. We would blow I-love-you kisses down the hallway, and there was no denying the deepening intimacy that was growing between us each day.

On a summer's eve, we would play music and dance in the kitchen or out on the deck while the grill heated up. I cooked, and he cleaned up. Then we would head out to the hammock after dinner, watching the leaves overhead as the gloaming crept in. Before bed, he would set up our cups and the coffee machine for morning. Nighttime fell, then another day dawned, and we started all over again. "Another day to love you" was our affectionate greeting each morning and throughout the day, which spoke of our devotion.

He planned a trip to Canada in late August to introduce me to his family. A good eleven-hour drive, we were both looking forward to it, and our time together in the SUV for our first big road trip. It did not even seem like a burden to spend that much time on the road; we always made it full of interesting talk or favorite music, and we were just happy to be together.

He introduced me to a little tourism promo song he knew from his youth and had fondly remembered. "A Place to Stand, A Place to Grow, We call this land Ontario, Ontario-o-o-o-o!"

I can just see him now, singing in the driver's seat as we got closer to the border belting out with sufficient animation "Ontario-o-o-o-o!" He was so proud of his Canadian roots, and their French name *Lefaive.* Only recently he became a US citizen so he could vote here but kept dual citizenship. He fondly remembered his father speaking French when they were children, and he loved his mother's French Canadian *tourtiere* meat pie and "butter tarts" for dessert. I attempted to make butter tarts for him once but failed miserably. We would make up for it with the real deal from a Canadian bakery on the trip—with or without raisins.

Before we left on the trip, he confessed to me that he wanted to book a hotel for a couple of nights in Niagara Falls and propose to me there. He knew it was a place well-known for engagements and weddings, just dripping with romance. I was touched by the sentiment, but there were snags. He had not yet met my daughters, and we had agreed to wait until after that milestone. Plus, we had just started shopping for the engagement ring. He was disappointed, but I was so moved that he had hoped to ask me at the falls, in his beloved Canada, and at the scene of its most natural wonder. That prompted more discussion about when our engagement *should* happen. We had booked the flight to Paris for mid-October to stay with Sharon and David, and it quickly fell perfectly into place. We would wait and get officially engaged in Paris. And the fairy tale dream continues!

I loved hearing about his childhood and life in Canada. His "Port McMichael" profile name, which I remembered from our first dating site contact, was in reference to his hometown of Port McNicoll, near Toronto. He played hockey for many years in school, was a good player, often the MVP. He kept his passion for the sport alive his whole life.

We had both been raised Catholic and compared our angelic first communion photos, all tattered and torn. Mine pictured me with my white dress and little veil held in place by a thin elastic band under my chin. White socks, shoes, and a little white purse completed the ensemble. Inside my purse was a tissue and my new white prayer book along with a guide to mass that we were all given for the special occasion. Michael's first communion picture showed him kneeling in church near the altar with black pants, a white shirt, and a little black bow tie. His hands were poised for prayer, and somewhere he had a similar little book for mass, as was given to me, but the boys' version was black. After serving as an altar boy, he attended a seminary and boarding school for a year in grade 9 (as they say in Canada). He admitted to me that he really just wanted to go there not so much to prepare for the priesthood but because they had such a good hockey team, and he wanted to be part of it! We were "cradle Catholics," and it showed as we both made the sign of the cross when we prayed, kept a crucifix near our beds, and well-remembered the custom of genuflecting before entering a church pew. Our Catholic heritage was just one more thing we had in common and brought us even closer.

One of four children, he explained that his parents had two babies before his father left for the war and two after he returned. The oldest were Betty and John, then later Michael came along followed by Larry, only eighteen months younger. Michael still displayed on his bookcase a framed eight-by-ten photo of him and baby brother Larry as toddlers, perched on a piano bench in matching overalls. So alike, some people mistook them for twins. Michael adored his older sister, Betty, who had died a few years before we met. Unfortunately, there was a falling out among the brothers over some inheritance issue, as happens in so many families. The three brothers could not agree, and consequently, Larry became estranged. Michael had not seen or heard from him in years.

Our visit with his family and his beloved Canada was all we hoped it would be. I was happily introduced to Tim Hortons donuts and coffee shops, and we made several visits. We did some shopping and came home with a dozen leaf-shaped bottles of *real* maple syrup as souvenirs. He drove me all over his hometown of Port McNicoll showing me their old house, schools, and where the church used to be before it burned down.

We visited his brother John and wife, Patricia, who still lived nearby. They greeted me warmly, and John and Michael had a lively conversation about "the old days." The brothers reminisced about the *SS Assiniboia*, a passenger and freight vessel which transported people and goods between Georgian Bay and the Canadian lake head near what is now Thunder Bay. A rich Lefaive family history began with their father Urbain (nicknamed Slim), who served as the second engineer for many years, later helping John and Michael get jobs onboard. John, being ten years older, worked full time for a few years before Michael got his first part-time summer job as a waiter and cabin boy. Larry was not yet old enough to apply when Michael began, and by the time he was of age, they no longer carried passengers, eliminating many jobs. Tragically, the ship burned in 1971 and was scrapped. The sister ship, the *SS Keewatin*, survived and was now docked at the harbor in Port McNicoll, open for daily tours.

The next day, Michael proudly escorted me around the restored vessel, furnished as it would have been in the fifties and sixties at its prime. In the classic formal dining room, we found a salvaged waiter's jacket on display, just as he wore so many years ago. I could just picture him in the stately black round-collared jacket with a row of brass buttons down the front and a big smile on his face. He recalled the all-male wait staff was strictly required to carry a tray of food and drink to the diners by balancing it only on fingertips, never using the palm of the hand. It was a skill he was proud to master. The *SS Keewatin* is the last surviving Edwardian ship in the world and was built five years before the *Titanic*. It is said that several of the *Keewatin* interior features were incorporated into the ill-fated ocean liner such as period deck chairs, hand-painted windows, and an ornate center staircase. Michael beamed as he interjected various facts and anecdotes to our tour guide and fellow guests from his unique perspective as a former crew member aboard the sister ship.

For the hometown reunion grand finale, we drove to a Toronto suburb to the home of his nephew Vince, son of John and Patricia. Vince and his wife, Julie, invited us for a delightful summer dinner along with several other family members so they could see Michael again and meet me. It was clear that Michael was a beloved uncle and brother and that his Canadian ties ran deep. I appreciated their warm hospitality and was delighted when as evening ended, one of his nieces said, "Welcome to the family, Gail."

The next morning, we were on our way to Niagara Falls, a wonder I had heard about all my life but had never seen in person. We passed a certain exit on the interstate, and Michael pointed it out, saying it was the town where Larry and his family lived. I felt a pang of distress for him and asked if he would try to reach out to his brother once again. Clearly, the wound still festered. He recounted the several times he had already tried but with no result. "Keep trying," I urged him silently, remembering these powerful words:

> Then Peter came up and said to him, "Lord, how often shall my brother sin against me, and I forgive him? As many as seven times?"
>
> Jesus said to him, "I do not say to you seven times, but seventy times seven." (Matthew 18:21–22 RSV)

The view of Niagara Falls from our room was magnificent, and we watched the fireworks and light show every night. We did all the touristy things including the boat ride in ponchos that went under the falls and viewing the incredible spectacle from the many observation stations. One day, we drove to Niagara-on-the-Lake, a nearby village, where we took an old-fashioned horse and carriage ride around town when we first arrived. I loved that Michael wanted to do that and seemed to enjoy it as much as I did. We had coffee and an *authentic* butter tart afterward at a sidewalk café, then browsed the many quaint shops along the main street just overflowing with hanging baskets full of late summer flowers in vibrant colors. We enjoyed a quick lunch in a quaint pub; then, we were on our way back for our final evening at the falls.

For the romantic culmination of the trip, he surprised me with reservations at a restaurant known for its impressive view of the falls. We had one of the best tables, with a clear view of the magnificent wonder at our fingertips. At the end of dinner when it was almost time for the nightly fireworks, he began expressing the most beautiful words imaginable about our future together. He then took my hand and pretended to put a ring on my finger and gently kissed it. Dropping to one knee with the illuminated falls and the incredible fireworks right outside the wall of glass, he promised to love and cherish me forever and asked me to be his wife. Michael got his Niagara Falls proposal, and I got an unforgettable memory.

We both felt so alive! We were thriving on each other's energy, enthusiasm, and love. True to our mutual intention to live life to the fullest, we kept right on making plans after our return from Canada.

Fall seemed like a perfect time to visit New England, so we flew into Boston, rented a car, and off we went. We stayed with my high school friend Kathy in Vermont doing some early leaf-peeping on the drive, marveling at the orange marmalade landscape mixed with a few dollops of grape jam. Next, we caught a couple of nights near Boston, with my cousin Mary Ruth and her husband, Phillip, eating fresh apples picked at an orchard that morning, and enjoying cool afternoons on their wraparound porch under a blanket. Our final stop was three nights at an idyllic bed-and-breakfast on Cape Cod, A Little Inn on Pleasant Bay, the perfect setting for my birthday. The weather was ideal, and we found the charming historic seaside absolutely invigorating. We indulged in great seafood every chance we got, watched the fishing boats dock while sharing a cup of the celebrated black raspberry ice cream, and lingered by the firepit all bundled up after dark, stargazing as lovers do.

6

Happily Ever After

If ever two were one,
then surely we.
If ever man were loved
by wife, then thee;
If ever wife was
happy in a man,
Compare with me ye
women if you can.

—Anne Bradstreet

A Paris engagement? Could anything be more wonderful? Our friends and hosts David and Sharon were busy planning outings and activities, and we completely deferred to their advice and direction on all things Parisian. They knew how to navigate the metro, how to plan excursions, and where to get the best chocolate croissant in town. Best of all, they opened their home to us—a lovely two-bed-room apartment on the Left Bank. Michael and I adored spending time with David and Sharon and were so grateful for their gen-erous invitation. Even though we had both been to Paris before, it was all new again as seen through the lens of our new love. But the brass ring on this carousel ride was our engagement. We felt prepared and ready. On separate occasions in previous weeks, Michael and I met for lunch with Mary Evelyn and Amy. Both went predictably well, and the stage was set for future gatherings with them and their families. Scott, Niki, and Zac were similarly supportive and welcoming. We also had the love and backing of countless friends on both sides, cheering us on. We reveled in it! The engagement ring had been selected and was under Michael's careful guard. Most importantly, we felt sure about taking this step, sure about our love, and sure about our future together.

When Michael enacted his surprise mar-riage proposal in Niagara Falls, he asked the waiter to take pictures of the special moment on his phone. The waiter was a waiter, not a photographer, and the pictures were no good. This made us think about our Paris engagement. We decided we did not want to take a chance on that special moment, and oh, what a photo op! At Sharon's suggestion, I contacted a photographer we found online in Paris. We checked the weather, picked a day, and set up the shoot. Lana texted details for where and when to meet. A young Parisian girl, she had done this before and had an impressive route picked out for the late afternoon two-hour photo session. We would meet at the *Pont de Bir-Hakeem* at 4:00. The evening sun would be perfect.

It was a flawless fall day. The temperatures in Paris had been above normal all month, and it was upper seventies (°F) or low twenties (°C), as the locals would say. Forecast rain showers had not started. I picked out an eggplant midi dress with three quarter sleeves and a colorful scarf; Michael wore a fall sweater with khaki pants that blended perfectly. It was glorious! A beautiful dream come true. Lana was skilled and knew how to suggest the best pose. Soon after we started, we had our precious moment when he officially proposed, and this time, he put a *real* ring on my finger. Several unforgettable photos captured my joyous response. After that, it was all celebration!

We posed in front of the Eiffel Tower, the colorful Trocadero carousel, near a scenic bridge, at magnificent fountains, and lastly the *Jardin de Tuileries*. Michael and I were completely animated in the moment, both having come from such dark places, but we had survived, then endured, and now we were truly living again. I thought to myself, *This must be what a bird feels like, boundless and free, not even touching the ground.* We were soaring!

After the shoot, we walked with Sharon and David to the Hotel Meurice on *Rue de Rivoli* to celebrate. This was no random choice. My mother had met my father in Paris after the war, and I knew from her notes that one of their early dinners together was at this hotel. The doorman welcomed us in out of the light rain, which had held off until now. As we entered, we were incredibly impressed by the décor, including stunning antiques accented with richly colored fabrics and styles of another day. We were seated in the luxurious bar, enjoying music from a pianist at a nearby baby grand, soon accompanied by a clarinet. We raised our glasses filled with their signature whiskey sour cocktail and toasted good friends, new love, and second chances.

Our celebration dinner was held at the Louvre's elegant Café Marley. Seated under the portico, we marveled at the tall arches of this grand architectural treasure. With the illuminated pyramid in view, we enjoyed an exceptional dinner with dear friends as this memorable day in our lives narrowed to its end. The experience had been a dream come true, and most importantly, we were now officially engaged!

Our Paris jaunt was drawing to a close, and we could not have asked for more. Our hosts were most accommodating, planning day-long visits at museums, the Seine river cruise, a visit to Notre Dame Cathedral, and an unforgettable day trip to Monet's Giverny. Even walking through the streets was a delight just peering into the bakery windows at such sumptuous works of art. The open-air markets were magnificent with their fresh fish and vegetables as mimes and accordion players entertained the shoppers.

A highlight of the trip for me was tracking down my grandparents' apartment on the *Champs Élysées* where they lived when I visited at age five and again at age ten. My grandfather, a poor farm boy from Georgia, went to Paris during WWI where he met and married my French grandmother, "the prettiest girl in Paris." After the war, he worked at the American embassy and decades later would eventually achieve the rank of US consul general during the Kennedy years. He could walk to his office at the embassy from this apartment on the first floor. I had the address and a photo of my mother and me standing outside the front door when I was a child. It looked somewhat different of course than it did in the 1950s, but the number was the same, and it was recognizable. It conjured up a memory of my walking with my granddad as a little girl down to the bakery to get a baguette before dinner. On the way back, he picked up a newspaper and stuck it up under his arm with the fresh baguette, his other hand holding mine.

Upon returning to North Carolina, our transition to a committed couple accelerated. Michael's condo in Greensboro went on the market and sold in a few weeks. He gave most of his furniture to his kids, and we gradually moved the rest of it to Chapel Hill, marking the beginning of our time here together.

We spent Thanksgiving Day at Amy's with extended family and friends and enjoyed their bountiful congratulations on our recent engagement. It felt so good to be at a family holiday as an official couple, with a wedding date just a few months away. In December, for the first time in years, a Christmas tree adorned the house, with all the trimmings. In fact, there were *two* trees! Seeing those sparkling lights twinkling again after so long filled me with such joy I was surely sparkling as well. We got tickets to some local holiday shows earlier in December and truly enjoyed the festivity of the season. It even snowed one weekend, to my delight, not his!

Our favorite holiday traditions blended beautifully, and we invited Michael's children here for gifts and a festive dinner. We loved being part of Amy and Don's Christmas Eve, complete with an early children's program at their church to see the Christmas pageant featuring angels with gold tinsel halos and shepherds with dish towels on their heads. Later that evening at their home, more of Don's family joined us for their traditional holiday spread. Mary Evelyn, Andy, and their kids arrived the week after Christmas for our family gift exchange and joint holiday feast, complete with snapping Christmas crackers at each place setting on the table and paper hats for all!

When our first Christmas morning arrived, it was just the two of us and just heavenly. The fireplace was blazing, the sparkling Christmas lights and candles added warmth to the ambience; we were cozy and perfectly content. We exchanged a few small gifts, and among mine was a monogram necklace with my new initials, which I would proudly wear in just a few months. I played Christmas carols on the piano, and Michael delighted in hearing me play, even with the inevitable mistakes. He would pull up a chair and sit next to me while I tickled the ivories, singing along, and cheering me on. Appreciating how hard holidays had been for both of us the last few years made this one all the more precious. Our wish list was short and sweet. What we desired was too big to fit in a stocking or under the tree. We wanted just one thing, and we wanted the same thing. On this blessed Christmas Day, we had each other, we were no longer alone, and that was the greatest gift of all.

We welcomed the New Year with great anticipation. In just a few months we would be married and the thought was exhilarating. We recognized that this new relationship was unique to us and unlike our earlier marriages. We both had good relationships with our late spouses, which is probably what encouraged us that we might find love again. But this was not same song, second verse. It was an original score made just for us. Being at a different place in our lives allowed us to concentrate on each other and our love. Instead of being caught up with career issues, financial concerns, or raising children and getting them through college, we landed in a very sweet spot. We just wanted to be together and take care of each other.

Our two SUVs seemed redundant, so we decided to trade mine in for a little silver-blue Volvo hardtop convertible. This demonstrative statement truly represented our unmistakable vim and vigor. We are alive, and we are living! Put the top down, turn the music up, and let's go for a drive! To break it in, we drove to Florida to spend the weekend with my friend Sarah who had always told me that January was a great time to visit. Like kids with a new toy, we could not get enough of riding with the top down, as we traveled the interstate with the music blaring and the wind in our hair. Sarah and her husband, Lee, showed us all around Orlando, then just the two of us went to Disney World for one magnificent day. I had not been to anything that resembled an amusement park in so long I could not remember, and to be there with my fun-loving Michael was as they say, "magical." It was indeed "The Happiest Place on Earth," and we were likely the happiest people there.

Greeting cards for every little anniversary or "just because" showed up as Michael hid them around the house where I would happen upon them with pure delight. On the envelope, he always wrote "My Gail" and sometimes would break into song with the old Temptations's hit, adapted for me. "My Gail, My Gail, *My* Gail, talking 'bout *My* Gail."

I would sincerely offer in return, "Thank you for loving me."

"Easiest thing I've ever done!" would be his swift reply.

One of my favorite cards began with the words, "Love of my Life" on the front, followed inside with touching sentiments. Even though we wish we could have met sooner, now it seems we found each other in just the right place and at just the right time. The sweet words declared that true love is always worth the wait, and that he would have waited forever for what we shared. Again came the proclamation that I was the love of his life and he signed it,

Love you, My Gail, with all my heart!
Michael XOXO

Nuptial plans took center stage, and the date was set for a garden wedding at home during the peak of early spring. By April 13, the dogwood and red bud trees should be in full bloom accented by the dozens of red, pink, and white azaleas at their feet. Early growth on numerous Japanese maples would light up the rest of the woodland. Brilliant Spanish bluebells, native coral columbines, and several of the early bearded irises would fill the beds with texture and color. At last, this garden, which I had loved for decades, was going to love me back by offering a perfect and personal place for our wedding.

We picked out the invitations and worked on the guest list. I suggested we send one to his brother Larry and his wife. Michael was reluctant, and I let it go. We sent one to his older brother, John, and wife, Patricia, and also several other Canadian family members, hoping some would be able to make the trip.

Details were taken care of for the caterer, the big white tent over the back terrace, the chairs, tables, linens, musicians, and wedding cake. We met with Margaret, our interim pastor, and planned the ceremony. She walked the garden with us as we chose the elevated spot where we would exchange our vows. The garden would be in its full spring glory, as we welcomed the most important people in our lives to help us celebrate our union. We could almost see the happy faces, hear the violins, and taste the sweet raspberry-filled wedding cake. Margaret led us as we reviewed our vows, and a hint of the joy that would surround us that day crept in, a joy we could hardly imagine.

I designed a few outdoor decorations using an old bolt of tulle that was wasting away in my sewing closet. Sequined ribbons left over from my daughters' weddings would add a little sparkle here and there. A tulle remnant was used to craft a rustic wedding veil for the three-foot-tall cement bunny in the garden, complete with a pearly tiara made from a holiday decoration. The three-tiered wedding cake would be topped with fresh flowers and displayed in the gazebo with swags of tulle and ribbon at each entrance, blowing softly in a warm breeze.

We made one last trip to the jewelry store to order our wedding bands. Michael was fond of recalling that I suggested "How about tomorrow?" on our first date. He often told me it was the best thing I could have said and meant so much to him. Our sales consultant, Karoline, asked if he wanted an inscription in his ring. He thought for a moment then lit up and said, "Yes! I want it to say 'How about tomorrow?'" Now those sweet words represented all the fond tomorrows of our dreams.

For Christmas, we had been given a Paris calendar for 2019, and Michael methodically marked off the one hundred days before our April wedding. As each day passed, he ceremoniously put a big X to cross it out, then proudly announced to me how many days remained. As we inched closer and closer, our excitement grew. I ordered a floor-length dress in a soft pink, and he was fitted for his tux choosing a pink bowtie and pocket scarf to match. Each step that brought us closer to the wedding day just made us happier, and we truly could not wait to be married.

The days neared, and the weather prediction worsened. We kept hope that our dream wedding could be realized all the way until the morning of the long-awaited day. It had rained heavily overnight, which was bad enough. We awoke before dawn and read the updated forecast for the day with disbelief. "Heavy rain with high wind gusts and possible flash flooding" spelled our doom. We would have to move it all inside. I was deeply disappointed, but Michael did his best to cheer me up, telling me it would still be wonderful, and that most importantly, we would be married at the end of the day. That was all the encouragement I needed. This dear man and I would soon be man and wife, and *that* was the prize.

Michael, Scott, and Zac quickly moved some furniture to the garage to create more open space in the living room, then moved smaller items to our bedroom. Niki and I walked back to the garden during a break in the rain and cut flowers for my bouquet. I had planned to have whatever was in bloom on the very day and whatever that was would be perfect. I clipped a few sprigs of lilac, a couple of yellow tulips, and some late white narcissus. The tulle and ribbon decorations my sister and I had put out the day before on the gazebo and the gate entrances were drenched and flattened. The cement wedding bunny's little veil with her pearly headband had blown away. Puddles of water were everywhere, and the sky was ominous. I could not look any more.

The photographer arrived early to take family group pictures, all now being taken in the living room instead of our glorious spring garden. The musicians were setting up and practicing from the second story loft by the staircase where the ceremony would be held. Instead of the grand display in the gazebo with tulle and ribbons adorning each entrance, the magnificent wedding cake topped with a blinking Eiffel Tower was placed on a small round table and shoved into a corner to make room for the guests. The caterers set up in the garage and worked their magic including freshly made French fries for the poutine bar and a selection of Southern delicacies to represent both our traditions. Michael's office was turned in to the bar, and the dining room table was pushed to a wall for the main buffet.

Our extended families arrived, some meeting for the first time. The wedding party, including our kids and my grandkids, waited upstairs as the guests entered. The rain was heavy, and wet umbrellas lined the front porch. Parking out front was difficult, and later, three tow trucks were needed. But our cheerful guests came in with smiles, many predicting it is good luck to get married in the rain, something I had never heard before. I later learned more about the saying which is credited to Hindu traditions. It is said that if a knot gets wet, it becomes exceedingly difficult to unravel. Similarly, if a couple "ties the knot" of marriage in the rain, their union would be just as hard to undo. Was it good luck? It was without a doubt the best luck ever that we met on that St. Patrick's Day just over a year ago, that we saw in each other the possibility of the love we longed for, that we followed through on our hunch that we would be so right together. And yes, it was good luck that over 150 loved ones came together to share our joy and our special moment. It was good luck that they could all squeeze in and shoulder to shoulder witness our vows and thereby inspirit us. It was not what we planned, but it was certainly lucky. We found our pot of gold.

The joyous moment arrived. Our dear friend and pastor, Margaret, opened the wedding ceremony with these apropos words:

> The prophet Isaiah compares the word of God to the rain that falls from heaven and brings the earth into bloom. Surely this is a magnificent place to imagine such love as the rain falls all around.
>
> She continued,
>
> Michael and Gail, we come rejoicing that you have found each other and opened your hearts to new possibility. As the world blossoms all around us, we give thanks that life comes back—to our gardens, and to our hearts.

After the ceremony, the music started, everyone clapped, and we slowly descended from the landing of the stairway, where the

ceremony had been held. Our family, standing on the upper steps and railing, showered
us on the way down with golden, glittered
hydrangea petals from our garden. A glorious
moment that embodied the phrase, "You can
just feel the love."

The party began, and how we celebrated!
The joy was palpable, and we could not stop
smiling. Eventually, the rain tapered off, and
guests ventured outside to the *après la pluie*
garden. We cut the cake and danced our dance
and reveled in the outpouring of love and support. Well-wishers told us over and over that
our love was so evident it made them happy
just to see us together. Some wedding guests
told us not only were they happy for us, but
they also said, "You deserve it." I heard this
well-meaning phrase, but in my heart, those
words did not ring true. Michael and I did not
deserve this *any more* than anyone else. Every
person deserves to be loved, cherished, and
made to feel special. We were just the lucky
ones. And we knew it. Perhaps it seemed we
beat the odds somehow, and our loved ones
shared in this joyous victory lap with us. We
represented a win, and everyone loves a win-

ner. Michael and I had come out of our darkness, into this light, and others felt the warm glow. They were loving us and lifting us up and, by doing so, became an important part of our happily-ever-after.

In the days that followed, we floated down from our cloud, grateful for so many blessings. We spent time digesting the incredibly beautiful wedding cards, which delivered evocative messages, often repeating a theme. *"Life is meant to be shared"* resonated loud and clear. *"Two are always better than one"* echoed strongly. Even an old Swedish proverb declares, *"Shared joy is double joy; shared sorrow is half sorrow."* It seemed the world, our world, meant to bless us with this message. We had been alone, we had been just one, but now joined together, we faced the rest of our lives with the promise of this precious gift of companionship. We were truly so happy to have each other to share this beautiful life with at last. One of our favorite cards sang out a reminder that *love can dare us to believe again and take another chance.*

We dared to believe again and took another chance, and now joyfully we were two, who became one. Our Caribbean honeymoon cruise was a perfect way to celebrate this new oneness. When we arrived at our cabin, we were greeted with a bottle of champagne chilling in an ice bucket. Nearby we found two stemmed glasses, a plate of chocolate-covered strawberries, and a note of congratulations from the staff. Later, we met our butler, Carlos, who presented us with several gift certificates from my college friends for us to use on excursions. I was "Mrs. Lefaive," and I reveled in it! We were here to celebrate our new marriage, and celebrate we would. Michael loved to ask people to take our picture; then, he would excitedly tell our fellow cruisers that we just got married. We delighted in the typical surprised reaction, followed by their congratulations. The brilliant sun and sea, the live reggae music, the piña coladas, the decadent restaurants and shows—what a celebration! After dinner the first night, the waiter proudly presented to us a small cake with a flickering candle and the words, "Happy Honeymoon."

It was just as heavenly to arrive home and begin our married lives together at last. With the details of the wedding and honeymoon behind us, we savored each quiet, ordinary day. "Another day to love you!" we would tenderly say to each other. Michael was back at work three days a week from his home office, filling prescriptions and treating addiction patients via tele-psychiatry. I got busy with the details of changing my name to Lefaive and applying for a new passport. With my lifetime airline passes, for which he was now eligible as my husband, we could not wait to get started on our travel bucket list.

The honeymoon trip had been so gratifying, that Michael insisted we go ahead and book our dream cruise to the Mediterranean, about which we fantasized on our second date. We would celebrate my seventieth birthday onboard in late September. Michael reserved a luxurious suite with a balcony, and the ten-day itinerary included several ports in Italy and two days in Barcelona. He picked out several incredible excursions to increase the decadence. We could not have been more exuberant about this trip of a lifetime. We booked the flight to Rome, and just to be safe, we bought the trip insurance.

The spring garden was fading, but early summer bloom burst forth with a fresh glory. Bearded iris, along with blue and white roof iris, and purple Japanese iris added spots of color to the emerging blue and pink heavenly hydrangea background. Michael became more and more interested in helping with the garden. I loved having his support in that way and loved his enthusiasm about it even more. He had not ever been a gardener per se, but he loved it and wanted to learn more. We were in the garden every day, walking the paths, resting on the hammock, sitting by the firepit, and always talking, sharing, communing. We would look at each other and look around, feeling so grateful for our circumstances and mostly that we found each other. We were so happily compatible and getting closer every day.

I kept busy tending my sixty-five hydrangea shrubs, which were in full bloom now and putting on a show. After cutting an armload,

I conditioned the stems to keep them from wilting. Later, arrangements were created to be enjoyed indoors as well as out. A big vase full of the luxurious blossoms graced the table on the deck near the porch swing. Eventually, the cut and dried mopheads could be used on a wreath or some winter arrangement. Hydrangeas were my favorite flower with their delicate petals and magnificent spectrum of color between pink and blue with shades of purple mixed in, depending on the soil pH. Like children, I know we should not have favorites, but I must acknowledge that in the hierarchy of southern plants, the hydrangea claims royalty. She is *queen*, and when in bloom, all else pales in comparison.

In the tradition of naming one's garden, I had tried but for years unsuccessfully identified any word that seemed to fit. Finally, after concentrated effort, I decided on the name *Belvedere*, which means "gazebo" in French. The name had to have some representation of the gazebo, my little crown jewel, nestled back in the woodland. My gazebo was the focal point and the heart of the garden, in both its central placement and for entertaining. Countless gatherings had been held there, including some very girly finger-food luncheons with chilled soups, cheese plates, and cucumber sandwiches. It was also perfect for *hors d'oeuvres* with wine and good friends in early evening. One year, when my granddaughter Ella Kathryn was about five years old, we even hosted a Fancy Nancy party for her in the gazebo, welcoming the neighborhood children to join in. Not that my garden was as grand, expansive, or impressive as many others with a well-known name, but it was more a part of my Southern culture to personalize this unique place, which was so special to me and to my many garden friends who often came to visit. Naming it somehow elevated it in a way which seemed appropriate. Now I could say, "You are invited to Belvedere" or have a sign bearing the words, "Welcome to Belvedere!" And it was somehow whimsical in the occasional magazine, news article, or social media post for the *jardin* to be referred to by name.

My beloved Chapel Hill Garden Club of which I had been a member almost twenty-five years was scheduled to hold their annual Spring Picnic at Belvedere in June. The date of the picnic would coincide beautifully with the peak of hydrangea season. Having served as president of the garden club for a couple of years early on, I was subsequently active in many roles. Claiming a membership of well over one hundred men and women, these were the smartest, most generous, and talented gardeners ever, and I was proud to be good friends with many of them. When the picnic chairman, Daphne, and her committee came to make the plans, I told them with a bit of sadness how our wedding cake was to be displayed with grandeur in the colonial gazebo for our reception before the rains came and the ceremony was forced inside. They sensed my deep disappointment and paid me the greatest favor by coming up with a new idea. It was the club's tradition that the board of directors provide several items for an assorted dessert display at the picnic. But this year, they would do something different—just for me. They all chipped in to buy a very expensive three-tiered cake, similar to our wedding cake and made by the same wonderful lady, who knew the story about getting rained out. We would reenact having the extravagant wedding-like cake in the gazebo, just as it would have been at our garden wedding.

The day of the picnic arrived, and just as with the wedding, rain threatened to move it inside. But overnight, there was a clearing, allowing us to set up in the garden after all. Tracy, the cake lady, arrived to deliver and decorate the cake, displayed elegantly on a footed silver riser. Frosting colors were selected to blend with my hydrangeas, and the cake was decorated at the last minute with fresh sprigs of these glorious blooms in the full array of pink, purple, and blue for the crowning glory. The guests arrived, and the ladies wore colorful, decorated garden hats as was our tradition, with a potluck salad in one hand and items for the auction in the other. The turnout was impressive, and we were seated at cloth-covered tables with chairs placed around the gazebo, just as it would have been at the wedding. The auction and the picnic lunch proceeded, and finally, it was time for dessert.

Michael and I said a word of thanks to everyone for coming, and especially to

Daphne, the picnic chairman, and her committee, for giving us the touching gift that
meant so much. We stood in our beloved
gazebo and cut a beautiful, tiered, culinary
confection, as we had so hoped to do at our
wedding. For some thoughtful gifts of friendship, there are no words big enough.

As our daily routine took shape, I discovered another newfound joy—being in the
kitchen again. Cooking had been dead to me,
and only for survival. Cooking for one—just
me—was totally void of the maternal and
domestic satisfaction I had known in preparing meals for Mike and my family. Lean
Cuisines or some bare minimum effort was
all I could muster for years. But with Michael,
it was all new again. I dusted off recipes for
several of my old favorites and reinvented my
culinary persona. For me, planning interesting and tasty meals was a way to express my
love for him. My new husband had a serious
sweet tooth, and I made desserts as never
before. The first pie I made him had the letter

M cut into the crust to allow steam to escape. A simple thing, but he was so touched by it. It was endearing to see his reaction. He knew I wanted to please him with my cooking, and he reciprocated by doing all the cleanup. "That's the least I can do," he insisted.

A satisfying feeling of normalcy and order was settling in. We had established a lively social life and often met up with local friends for a drink or dinner. The usual couple invitations started to come in, and we were happy to oblige. In fact, we loved it! We saw our friends from Southern Pines and Paris fairly often and were really bonding. Michael was genuinely social, and he naturally attracted friends. We attended church every Sunday that we were in town and were making more and more contacts there as well. That was a whole other pool of people who wanted to meet this friendly, smiling guy. The neighbors on our street often stopped to say hello, and things felt right. We saw Niki, Zac, and Scott from Greensboro on a regular basis and also Amy and family as often as possible. Amy's boys were now nine and six and filled a special place in Michael's heart as he had not yet been blessed with his own grandchildren. He was crazy about them, and each hello and goodbye was filled with smiles and affectionate hugs.

Being an early riser, Michael often got up before me and worked at his desk until the smoky light of dawn tiptoed past the dark. Often when I finally got up after our sumptuous early morning mingle, I would be delighted to find he had turned on the accent lighting in the kitchen and bookcases, and music was softly playing. On a frosty morn, the fireplace was lit, taking off the chill. Deep feelings of warmth, well-being, and contentment overcame me as I savored these blessings from this dear man.

To say we were still on our honeymoon would be an understatement. The simplest tidbits of everyday life were more joyful just because we were together. We felt silly and giddy, and our faces hurt from smiling. One hot Saturday in late July, we headed over to the nearby farmers market to buy some fruit for breakfast. We happily discovered it was "Tomato Day," a local celebration for tasting the summer delicacies, and we patiently waited in line for our turn to sample the bounty. Heirlooms like German Johnson, Cherokee Purple, and Homestead tomatoes crowded the display table in bite-size pieces, with a few Celebrity and Early Girls thrown in for good measure. Toothpicks were everywhere! We savored the warmed-by-the-sun sweetness, the hint of purple, and the undeniable unique flavor that makes these magnificent gifts of the garden so desirable and celebrated. With a fresh cantaloupe, two pints of blackberries and oodles of local love apples, we headed home. Our tummies and hearts were full, and we felt satisfied in body and soul at the true, simple goodness of the morning and the true simple goodness of our love.

We had been together a little over a year, and our young marriage was blissful. We told each other we have lots and lots of years ahead together, and there was no reason to think otherwise. Now with the frenzy of the wedding behind us, we had settled into the comfortable warm place of simply and joyfully being together. We seemed to be living our ideal life, and for that, we never stopped being grateful. I had spent years thinking I could never love again, but instead, I found more love than ever—our growing family, our home and garden, the church, and the true love of a good man. After such pain for both of us, losing our longtime spouses and managing the difficult years that followed, we had found each other and found happiness. This was our dream come true. We could take a deep breath. The worst was behind us now. We made it!

7

A Light in the Darkness

*The light shines in
the darkness,
And the darkness
Has not overcome it.*

—John 1:5 (RSV)

Sometime around June, Michael noticed a wheezing in his breath. He would have it checked at his upcoming physical. A couple of weeks later, a CT scan showed he had pneumonia, which they would watch, and he would have it tested again in a month. But disturbingly, it also showed some "spots" on his bones. After the phone call from his doctor with this news, we were both stunned. I tried to think of something encouraging to say, but it threw me right off balance. We stood together just looking at each other in disbelief. I stuttered, "Don't make me cry," and he replied, "Don't make *me* cry!" But we did. We stood there feeling the fear descend upon us. We just held each other and cried.

Clearly, this was fraught with trepidation. We were scared but did our best to comfort each other and wait out the agonizing weeks until his next appointment. Was this going to be the end, so soon? We just got started! We had so much to live for! The new scan confirmed bone cancer but a type that was treatable with a targeted chemotherapy. The chemo pill would prevent new cancerous growth, and it would not be life-threatening. He would not even lose his beautiful silver hair! We were overjoyed at another second chance. We were grateful beyond words and excitedly resumed our growing love affair.

Buoyed by this positive development, he wanted to celebrate. In typical Michael style, we booked a last-minute cruise around Mexico for July and kept right on living. Once again, we were spoiled with the ship's elegant accommodations, indulgent food, and top-notch entertainment. The everyday scenery was spectacular and competed with the delectable cuisine for top billing. It was a true dining sensation with entrées like broiled lobster, beef wellington, chateaubriand, then ending with cherries jubilee or flaming Baked Alaska to name a very few. Cruising was his favorite travel mode, his authentic *modus operandi*, and he embraced it, as active and vibrant as ever. He loved the excitement of being on deck for each departure and arrival. We had access to the *retreat deck* for sunning, which included beautiful cabana-type lounges and elaborate hot tubs with big fluffy towels. The friendly staff regularly delivered tropical rum concoctions and *hors d'oeuvres* including our favorite treat—a shot glass of chilled champagne served with a tiny cup of frosty raspberry sorbet. The flavor sensation exploded in the hot sun as we basked in the decadence of both our adventure and the joy of our deepening love.

Michael was the epitome of friendliness and openness to others. A kind word of praise or appreciation was always on his lips. He did not hesitate to ask others to take our picture, which usually led to a longer conversation about where they were from, were they cruisers, etc. And always that smile—that bright, beautiful smile! I did so love his outgoing personality because I knew it was so genuine, so him. On the flight home, we did not have seats together on the airplane and met up with each other near the jet bridge door after landing. I asked him if he made a new friend during the flight, and he replied, "Six!"

His breathing was close to normal, and he easily participated in all cruise activities except snorkeling. We were not terribly worried about the pneumonia since he was not even advised to seek medical treatment. Actually, we felt encouraged at the prognosis, which allowed us to continue to enjoy our newlywed status. Soon after we returned home, Michael had another lung x-ray and was told there was not much change. He would wait and test again in another month.

A couple of weekend trips ensued, including a fifteen-mile biking adventure that he managed without a hitch. From our point of view, he was doing well. The third lung x-ray showed only a slight change, and no one seemed alarmed, but he was advised to make an appointment with a pulmonary specialist to check it out. The soonest he could be seen was the end of August. Michael wanted to get in one more trip before this next step, so we threw together a Banff getaway.

Neither of us had ever been to Lake Louise, and it was high on our list. By the time we arrived, he was starting to slip. We wondered if being at the high altitude had somehow compromised his breathing. It came on so fast. We were traveling on my airline passes and got the last two seats in first class between Chicago and Calgary. He told me it was his first time ever to be in first class, but he could not even enjoy it and even passed up the hot-plated lunch and dessert. When we arrived at our picturesque hotel on the main street in Banff, he collapsed on the bed, feeling weak and drained. Later we decided to venture out to the nearby grocery store for supplies, but he had to stop to rest at every bench we passed. We went to dinner in the hotel restaurant, and he ordered a cup of tomato soup. I encouraged him to take a few spoonsful, but he shook his head, saying, "I just can't." We could not understand what was happening, but he wanted to proceed with our sightseeing plans. We had come this far, and we were determined to see that incredible blue water of Lake Louise with our own eyes. The next day, he drove the rental car without difficulty, and things seemed somewhat better. He ate very little but surprisingly had the stamina to do the hiking required to see the sights. Being athletic all his life and in good shape before this hit was paying off. The natural beauty of this area was so impressive, we were truly overwhelmed. Everything we had ever heard or seen about Banff and Lake Louise was true, and then some. He was so proud of his native Canada and so proud to show it off to me.

We saw the pulmonary specialist within a couple of days of our return. Dr. Patel did a complete workup on Michael and ordered a CT scan and some other tests including a bronchoscopy to retrieve a tissue sample for a biopsy to rule out lung cancer. Michael told him excitedly about our ten-day

Mediterranean cruise scheduled for the end of September, explaining that he had to get better and soon! Dr. Patel expressed doubt that he could recover in time for the cruise, which was very hard for Michael to hear. We were disappointed, but the greater priority was his health. We could always schedule another cruise.

A week later when Michael arrived for the biopsy at the hospital, his oxygen saturation level was so low they cancelled the bronchoscopy and immediately admitted him to the ICU. The high-dose supplemental oxygen available only in the ICU was just what he needed, and after six days, his appetite returned, and he was getting stronger. He enjoyed conversing with the staff and in particular bonded with a nurse named Christine. Their common interest was travel in Canada and Europe and, of course, good food. He seemed in very good spirits and to be recovering well as we did our best to calm concerns of worried family members.

The ICU team agreed on the diagnosis of a rare lung condition called COP or cryptogenic organizing pneumonia. On day four or five, one of the doctors came in and said to him, "Mr. Lefaive, you do not belong in the ICU." We were thrilled at the positive assessment and could not wait to get out of there. They decided the bronchoscopy would be too hard on him now, and they no longer suspected lung cancer, so he never had the biopsy. He would be discharged and on portable supplemental oxygen for a few weeks while he healed. A home health nurse came and offered exercises and advice on coping. We were going home. Hope rescued us again.

He did his exercises faithfully to build strength, and things progressed. It was so hard to cancel the cruise, but we knew it was for the best. My birthday plans could be rearranged. We filled out and submitted the necessary forms for the cancellation refund. Dr. Patel provided a letter with the details of Michael's illness to authenticate our claim. With things so tentative, I cancelled our hotel reservations for the Emory and Henry Homecoming scheduled for mid-October, and we dropped our plans for a fall weekend trip to visit apple orchards in the North Carolina mountains. As much as I hated to do this, I was convinced he would continue to improve as the doctors suggested, and we would reschedule these activities next autumn.

My seventieth birthday was coming up at the end of September, and Michael felt so badly that his illness was responsible for our change of plans. I would not be blowing out the candles in Italy as we had hoped. To compensate, he insisted on buying me a digital baby grand piano, an extravagant but loving gift. Currently and for the first time in my life, I was without a piano. Just a few months before, I had given my beloved Gaveau to my daughter Amy whose boys had recently started piano lessons. It was time. I wanted them to grow up playing that special piano just as my two daughters had and as I had and as my mother had before me. It was a blessing to have enjoyed it all these years. It was not a Steinway and had started to show its age, but it had been in the family almost a hundred years and was a true heirloom. Michael knew how much I missed my piano and how hard it was to let it go. He wanted to fill that void with this generous birthday gift. Such a loving, thoughtful gesture coming from him with such sincerity made it all the more precious to me. It arrived a few days before my big day giving us time to assemble and place it.

We invited Amy's family, Niki, Zac, and Scott, along with our couple friends for my birthday party. After a round of margaritas, we enjoyed a Mexican fiesta potluck dinner on the garden terrace. The grandkids were playing in the treehouse and on the swing before they presented me with my favorite—their homemade birthday cards. Michael was seated with his oxygen nearby, full of smiles and enjoying the festivity. My friend Barbara, well-known for her exceptional cooking skills, had made the birthday cake, a *tres leches*—beautiful and delicious! They all sang to me as I happily blew out the three candles representing past, present, and future. In terms of my time with Michael, our past was brief and beautiful, our present was rich and satisfying, and our future seemed bright in spite of the recent weeks.

The doctors were hopeful that his COP would continue to improve with the home supplemental oxygen and some time to heal.

We were feeling positive about his recovery and our future together as we drank in the goodness of the food, music, and fellowship. The party ended back in the house with a little piano recital on the new "baby" to show it off. Amy and I started playing duets from years past, then Sam and Isaac performed their latest songs. All the while, Michael sat nearby, smiling proudly at his oh-so-perfect birthday gift. We were not on a Mediterranean cruise, but we were home, out of the dreaded ICU, and had an encouraging prognosis. That was the gift I really wanted—happy birthday to me!

The next morning was Sunday, and he seemed weaker. Perhaps it was the excitement of the birthday party and all the activity that wore him out, but that was normal, right? His oxygen saturation level, also known as "sats" remained low even with the supplemental oxygen. He had an appointment with Dr. Patel in a week. By Monday, we both knew he had to go in sooner. I called early, and they scheduled another CT scan for that afternoon; then, we would come in first thing the next morning, October 1. We were hardly in the clinic ten minutes before they determined he had to go right back to the ICU. His sats were way too low, alarmingly low. I drove him to the hospital emergency room entrance and waited with him until a room became available. *This wasn't happening.*

Our distress was mitigated briefly when we learned Christine was on duty and would be the nurse to admit him this time. Her friendly face and attentive care eased the transition and helped calm us both. Michael and I needed her reassuring words. Dr. Patel and the other ICU doctors continued to evaluate him and were disturbed at his decline. A lung biopsy was the next step and quickly ordered. He could not tolerate the bronchoscopy due to his labored breathing, so the only option was a needle aspiration through his back. The procedure was done in the first few days, followed by the long, terrifying wait for the results. His kids came to spend time with him and distract him. My sister Janine was here to help, and Mary Evelyn had just arrived from

Georgia, so he was rarely alone. We tried to wear a happy face, but we were all so scared.

John, my friend and pastor, came to visit from church and offer solace. He had been with our family during Mike's illness, and now, here we were again. I was deeply troubled by a sensation I was experiencing, or should I say *re-experiencing* after losing Mike. My burning question for John was, "How does one balance the fear and the hope at a time like this?"

He answered eloquently and reminded us that even Jesus prayed, "Father, let this cup pass from me." In my daze and despair, I knew he was speaking, but my emotions were too scattered to process his message. I saw his mouth moving, but the volume in my head was turned way down. I so desperately wanted and needed to hear his response, but I could not. All I remember him saying was that yes, both fear and hope will be present, but not to let the fear paralyze us or take over, and to always keep hope alive. Maybe that was all I could handle at this critical moment.

I would never let hope die! I would never give up. I believed that unexplained healing takes place in certain situations and that miracles do happen. I would never stop praying for our miracle that would bring him home again. I would pray that God would spare his life and give us what we wanted so desperately: more time together.

The three of us prayed, then as John was leaving, Michael asked him with tears in his eyes, "What's going to happen to Gail? She didn't sign up for this."

John responded, "Actually, she did."

We soon bonded with several of the nurses who rotated in and out. Christine was always a welcome familiar face and was joined by Caille, Beth, Sophie, and others composing our inner circle of favorites. They would sometimes ask to be his nurse for their shift, and if not, they would come by to visit and cheer him up.

One morning when I arrived at his room, I did a double take when I met our new nurse for the day. *Could it be?* I looked at her name tag. Yes, it was Adrienne, the same nurse on duty the day Mike died almost six years ago. I could never forget that sweet, caring face, and her announcement, "He has passed." It was indelibly written in my mind. I was stunned. She did not seem to recognize me, and I did not say anything. My new married name was different, and I had lost some weight in these past difficult years, so maybe she would not notice, and besides, she had families rotating in and out every day. She might not even remember me. I debated whether I should re-introduce myself to her or just let it be. Maybe it would be strange or awkward for her. Or maybe it would be strange or awkward for me. It was bad enough being in the same ICU and just down the hall from where Mike took his last breath. But now here I was again with my new husband. It was the same hospital, the same ICU, and now the same nurse. It was really too much *déjà vu*, so I let it slide. I never told Michael about Adrienne, about how she had been there in Mike's final moments. But he was well aware of the uncomfortable coincidence that he was now being treated in the same unit where Mike died, just a few rooms away. He kept apologizing to me that his illness was making me relive the trauma, as if he had any control over that.

One of my Catholic friends offered to invite their new priest to stop by our room when he was at the hospital making his own pastoral care rounds. Since Michael and I had both been raised Catholic, it felt right. We welcomed Father Chris who happened to come at a time when Niki and Zac were visiting Michael, which was a blessing. His delightful personality put us all at ease, and laughter filled the room. We did not expect anything more than an encouraging visit, a prayer, and a blessing, but soon he announced, "Michael, I will now administer to you the sacrament of the anointing of the sick." Michael and I looked at each other. We knew what that meant. When we were kids, it was called extreme unction, part of the last rites. We knew it to be something done at the suggestion of possible imminent death.

The sacrament had changed over the years to include anyone suffering from an illness of any kind, to provide blessings and support in any phase of sickness and not just for the deathbed. Still, it stung. Father Chris continued. He prayed for Michael and his return to health, then anointed his forehead and hands with holy oil. Special prayers were read from a small black book with red ribbon markers—beautiful prayers, inspiring prayers. Then we all stood around Michael's bed holding hands as Father Chris offered a blessing. We ended with the Lord's Prayer. We thanked Father Chris for coming and for his unexpected gift.

The biopsy results were in. A doctor we knew fairly well came in the room and quickly sat by the bedside. With a helpless look on his face, he took Michael's hand and uttered, "It's cancer."

There was that word. There was that dreaded word, that bully of a word: a word full of fear, full of oppression, full of intimidation. Riding on the back of that ominous word was a menacing stranger, threatening to steal away our second chance, threatening to steal away "another day to love you." The pneumonia diagnosis somehow felt survivable, but this apocalyptic threat fell hard on our hopeful hearts. Michael and I were visibly shaken. The oncology team would soon evaluate him and suggest a treatment plan. The kind doctor left, and Michael and I embraced, unable to hold back our tears.

Things got serious in a hurry. The oncologists were alarmed at his stage 4 condition. He was weaker, and his sats were not where they should be with this much supplemental oxygen. The next few days were crucial. He was past traditional lung cancer treatment; however, they informed us about a targeted chemo drug that would be promising for him, but only if he was a mutation match. They would take samples and submit them for evaluation immediately, but it would take up to nine days for results. We grabbed on to the hope.

A couple of days later, four members of the oncology team came into the room ominously, with a new plan. Reading between the lines, they feared he would not make it to the end of nine days, but since he was so highly motivated and otherwise functional, they reversed the earlier decision, allowing traditional chemo treatment. If he turned out to be a mutation match when results were in, they would be that much ahead of the game. They warned that Michael's breathing was so compromised that there existed the real possibility of his having a serious breathing event at any time and not surviving. If he made it through the weekend, he would get the traditional chemo on Monday.

Our emotions were all over the place. We were trying to stay hopeful and positive yet crushed by the evolving scenario. He had seen the grim faces on the oncology team, and he heard their inexorable prognosis.

Propped up in bed with tears rolling down his cheeks, he wondered out loud to me, "What if I don't ever get to come home again? What if we never get to make love again? What if I never get to see the boys again? I was so looking forward to watching them grow up." My heart was breaking.

He did survive the weekend, and the chemo treatment was administered on Monday as scheduled. He was wiped out for a couple of days then rallied. He actually seemed to improve, and we were infused with positive energy. He was eating a little, mostly milkshakes, and his spirits were back. Now we would wait another week for the results of the mutation match.

One day at a time.

Janine went home to Virginia, and Mary Evelyn stayed a few more days. She spent time with us in the ICU, took care of things at the house, and dropped me off at the hospital so I did not have to drive. Most of all, she was meaningful moral support for me at night when I would collapse after another long emotional day at Michael's side. Amy had developed a serious aversion to that same ICU where she sat for hours and days those short years ago watching her father weaken then die. She could not bring herself to enter those dreaded halls again, not even under these unusual circumstances. I understood and appreciated how she did so much to support me in other ways. During the day while the boys were in school, she would come and bring me food or whatever I needed. She would pick me up at the hospital; then, we would drive around as she helped me think things through and let me cry on her shoulder in disbelief that this was even happening.

My girls both offered such abundant support in my hour of need. What a blessing it is that each of us has our own particular gifts of the heart to give to one another in trying times, and they are as individual and unique as we are.

The staff at church had changed since my last ICU crisis. Our senior pastor Bob had retired and our associate pastor Anna had answered a call to a new church in West Virginia. John was still on board thankfully and had recently been joined by our new co-pastors Meg and Jarrett. Michael and I had been to church that summer Sunday when they were ceremoniously welcomed by the congregation, but travel and illness had prevented us from attending since then. I got a text from Meg asking if she could visit, so we met her in person for the first time in a hospital room, not in our sanctuary as we had imagined it. Michael was having a good day, and as usual, he delighted in telling the story of how we met, how we got engaged in Paris, and our whole wonderful love story. He charmed her with his wit and smile. We bonded immediately. Meg told Michael he was on the prayer list, and the whole congregation would be solidly in his corner.

October 13 was our six-month wedding anniversary. It was unconscionable to think that only six short months ago, we stood amid our dearest friends and family exchanging our vows and looking forward to being married and to taking care of each other. We were so sure it was going to be longer than this. I made sticky buns that morning, and we would celebrate today and hold fast to the possibility that things could turn around. I put the same little blinking Eiffel Tower that adorned our wedding cake on top of the gooey goodness and headed over. When I arrived, he smiled, said "Happy anniversary," and we shared a sweet kiss. Then he asked me to hand him a book from the table. When I did, I could see a paper sticking out of it and he said, "Go ahead, open it." There on a piece of folded printer paper, he had written with purple marker, "*Joyeux Anniversaire* to my wife, the love of my life," followed by, "You are Perfect to Me!" in green.

Inside, printed in red ink were these loving words:

> October 13, 2018—
> That memorable and joyous day in Paris.
> I asked, and you accepted my proposal of marriage.
> My heart sang on that day and it continues to sing more and more.
> You have fulfilled my needs and more.
> I love you, My Gail!!!

He joked about doing arts and crafts in the ICU and told how his night nurse helped by finding him some colorful markers to use.

It was mid-October, and we had now been in the ICU two long, chilling weeks. Canadian Thanksgiving Day arrived, which prompted us to write out our gratitude list. We would post it on Facebook for all to see and truly appreciate the positive things in our situation.

> In spite of all that is going on, we know we have so much to be thankful for: WE HAVE EACH OTHER; Michael is not in pain, there is no fluid retention, all his other organs are functioning properly, we are filled with hope, AND we are present and loving in each precious day. PTL!!

The oncologist came in a few days later with devastating news that results were back, and he was *not* a mutation match. Our hearts sank. There was an option for another possible match, and she would submit it quickly. It also had about seven to nine days turnaround, but at least, it was a chance. If he matched, this magic pill would start working quickly, and he would not lose his silver hair or have other typical chemo reactions. Again, we waited with hope.

My sister Janine came back and took over for Mary Evelyn who returned to her family in Georgia. Just as Mary Evelyn had been, Janine was a godsend, taking care of meals for us and everything at the house. She also drove me to the hospital and picked me up so I would not have to deal with parking and the long walk to the main entrance. Then she would return to be with us for a few hours each day. By this time, we had really bonded with several of the nurses, which Janine dubbed "Michael's Angels," and indeed they were. Janine brought them bakery cookies and took their pictures with Michael, always making sure they knew how much they were appreciated. Christine, Adrienne, Sophie, Beth, Caille, and Susan went above and beyond and truly earned their angel wings!

Part of Michael's treatment was to try to walk. The nurse would pack up his oxygen tank, follow him with a chair should it be needed, and off we would go. Just leaving his room and walking around the unit felt so good as he smiled and waved to everyone he saw. If he tired, he could sit and rest then continue. A couple of times, he would round a corner, and some familiar doctor or nurse would recognize him, start clapping to cheer him on, then others nearby would join in. Such amazing support from these incredible doctors and nurses! Everyone wanted him to win and survive, no one more than me. His recovery would be a victory for us all.

One evening when I was about to leave for home, we began to cuddle as we said good night. Christine entered and told us she had a surprise for us. Standing tippy-toe on a chair, this sweet woman stretched her arm high to tape a piece of paper over the camera in the ceiling so we could have privacy. No longer was our every move visible on the giant monitor at the front desk. Christine left after encouraging us to snuggle and be close. Lying down by his side, with a loving embrace, we held each other. No talking, just holding, just being.

A more desirable ICU corner room with a wall of windows opened up, and Adrienne quickly took steps to have Michael moved there. It was a shot in the arm, and the impact of hours of sun shining in was unmistakable. Friends and neighbors kept asking what they could do, and finally we responded, "Send a funny card." Our mailbox was overflowing in days! I would arrive each morning with a stack of cards for Michael to open and read with delight. We taped them all over the room and on the wide bright windows. Everyone who entered remarked how cheerful they were. Included were cards from his Canadian family, all of whom were wonderfully in touch and supportive. His older brother John called and texted frequently along with nieces and nephews. Facebook was full of messages flying back and forth about his condition. We kept learning of new prayer lists bearing his name, which made us so grateful, as we truly believed in the power of prayer. The cards reminded us how many friends and family were thinking of us, praying for us, and helping us through each trying day as we moved toward our nebulous destination.

Another ten days or so passed, and by this time, Michael could no longer walk. He was not eating at all and was so weak he could hardly sit on the edge of the bed and let his feet swing over. It was getting difficult for him to even sit propped up with pillows, something he did easily just a couple of weeks ago. I knew these were bad signs, but I also knew there was the outside chance that he would be a match for the second mutation trial and that his second chemo was coming up on November 1. If he could just make it till then, he could receive the life-giving meds.

Dr. Patel visited regularly to check on Michael and provide an encouraging word. Within the revolving door of doctors collaborating on Michael's care, he was the one constant. He promised to always be up front with us, but it was excruciating to hear from him that it was such a long shot. Finally, he put a number to it and estimated only a 10 to 20 percent chance of surviving until and after the second chemo. I trembled at the thought of sharing this dispirited forecast with Niki and Scott, knowing how it would undermine our communal hope. But honestly, I still held on to even that small chance, deeming it better than no chance at all. Michael had already done better than they expected in early October, so maybe he could continue to beat the odds? That was my prayer.

On that same day, Dr. Patel declared that intubation was now off the table, after we had spent the last few weeks debating the option. He concluded that with Michael's worsening condition, it would be a "bridge to nowhere." This was a blessing and a curse. An important therapeutic tool would now be unavailable to him. But reflecting on my own memories of Mike being intubated with the worst outcome, being told it had become only life support, I shunned the idea. This provided a sense of relief for me, plus Michael did not want to be in a state of intubation if the end came, rendering him unable to be present in the moment or communicate with his loved ones. Amen, so be it.

Amid all the downturns, there was this to be thankful for: he was not in pain. He had "air hunger," which is described as a feeling of drowning, unable to get a breath. They supplied him with a morphine pump that he could press when he was feeling anxious, but we all recognized the blessing that he did not have to suffer constant pain as do so many cancer patients. And at this point, we had to grab and appreciate every blessing we could find.

We entered a period of calm and waiting. There was a stillness, a peace, as if things were fine even though we knew they were not. We received a gift of what we wanted most—a little more time together, "another day to love you." It was a brilliant awareness of our sacred present moment. I thought back on my earlier question to Pastor John about how to reconcile the fear and the hope. Michael and I both needed the hope to survive each day and not to let fear win, not to let fear paralyze us. But fear was not the enemy, it was the other side of hope. I was starting to understand. In this sacred time, fear and hope join hands in love. The fear loosens its grip, the hope tempers with time, and what remains is love. It was the light of this love shining out into the darkness, "and the darkness has not overcome it" (John 1:5 RSV).

8

The Nightmare

Love is the greatest of dreams,
yet the worst of nightmares.

—William Shakespeare

Results of the second mutation match trial were due any day, and we approached the arrival of November 1 when Michael would have the second chemo treatment. Either or both would be a good thing. Doctors kept saying he was doing well considering his condition; his blood oxygen levels were acceptable, and they urged him to keep up the good work. We were advised to have visitors if he wished and to enjoy every day. With his social personality, he welcomed this. In the early weeks in ICU, we had only a few visitors other than clergy and family, but now the door was open. Even though he was weak, not eating, and unable to walk, his face would light up with the arrival of a friend or neighbor to brighten his day. Ever the gracious host! This was feeding his soul. This is what he needed and had missed. The visits fell into place without any effort on my part. I just released it, and it was perfect. It was beautiful. Extended family including my brother John and his wife, neighbors, former colleagues, new friends from church, and dear close friends he had bonded with, all came together to shepherd us through this nightmare.

One day, his cell phone rang, and the caller ID said Ontario, Canada. I showed it to Michael, and he looked at the number. "That would be Larry," he said with a smile. The doctor was in the room, so he could not take the call. Later, he listened to Larry's message. He had heard of Michael's illness and wanted to talk. I texted Larry and set up a time. These two brothers, toddlers on the piano bench, estranged for over five years were going to talk. When the time came the next day, I placed the call, and Larry answered. He and

Michael exchanged loving words, and they both shed tears. They talked about lost years and regret. They talked about misunderstandings and forgiveness. In a moment, it was all made well. The brotherly love was stronger than the quarrel and reigned supreme. The only regret was that it had taken this illness to make it happen.

Over the weeks, I read aloud to Michael. He would rest as I read, his weary eyes closed but our hands were always touching, and he would slowly and gently run his thumb across my fingers. He would touch my wedding ring and tell me how proud he was to have me as his wife. We had done an interview with a local magazine about our wedding a few months earlier, and the issue had just come out. There was a full-page story and photo of us in complete wedding garb as well as a group family photo. We got several copies to give the nurses and show people who came to visit. What a bittersweet remembrance of our special day.

Niki, Zac, and Scott came as often as they could. Working full time made that difficult, but they were always there on the weekends and several weeknights. The hour-long drive from Greensboro was a burden. Scott had written some poetry and read to his father with his commanding, soothing voice. Michael listened with pride and savored the time they were spending together. Niki lit up the room when she came in, and Michael's proud papa smile revealed his joy. He just adored his Niki, and she adored him right back. Zac, his new son-in-law, with his amicable and fun-loving spirit added so much to our visits. Niki and Zac made a handsome couple, and their devotion to each other gave Michael great satisfaction.

Suddenly, the period of calm and waiting was over. The oncologist came in late one day and announced solemnly, "He is not a match." Another stab in our wounded hearts. We had held such hope for this mutation match and now sensed an even deeper desperation settling in. But the option for the second chemo treatment was scheduled and now just a few days away. He had done well after the first treatment, and we had every reason to believe he would respond well again.

It was torturous to deliver this news to Niki and Scott, and we shared a growing despair. Options were running out, one by one. I posted this devastating update on Facebook to keep our circle of dear ones informed and implored for continued prayers. The outpouring of love and support was humbling. My dear friend Sarah sent me a scripture that bolstered my soul and stayed in my heart: "May the God of hope fill you with all joy and peace in believing, so that by the power of the Holy Spirit you may abound in hope" (Romans 15:13 RSV).

Prayers seemed to surround us, and we welcomed them all. One of the ICU doctors was a big burly fellow from Africa who was also an ordained minister. Dressed in casual blue scrubs, he came in after rounds one day and stood at the bedside. "Are you believers?" he asked. We both nodded yes, and he replied, "I thought so." He said, "I would like to read some scripture with you later, if you would like." Michael agreed, and I took a picture of them with the doctor leaning down to his bed, both smiling widely. Before he left the room, he took Michael's hand in his and said, "You know we are related. We have the same Father."

A few days later, he returned and with his phone, pulled up the verses. He read the words with deep feeling and expression.

> For I am sure that neither death, nor life, nor angels, nor principalities, nor things present, nor things to come, nor powers, nor height, nor depth, nor anything else in all creation, will be able to separate us from the love of God in Christ Jesus our Lord. (Romans 8:38–39 RSV)

Then with great exhilaration, he added, "Isn't that wonderful news? Nothing will ever separate us from the love of God, nothing! Michael, you are a child of God, and His love is forever. Will you pray with me?" I joined hands with them both, and we bowed our heads. With his heavy Cameroon accent, he began, "Heavenly Father, thank You for the gift of eternal life. Thank You for the gift of everlasting love. Bless and hear the prayers of Your servant Michael. We know that if You want to heal him, Lord, it would be so easy for You. May Thy will be done. In Jesus's name we pray, amen."

Michael was not afraid to die. He told me he was at peace and knew he would be in heaven. We often prayed together, and both made the sign of the cross, a tradition from our Catholic roots. I wish now I could have been able to share with him these profound words from Henri Nouwen on the subject so hard to discuss.

> Preparing ourselves for our deaths is the most important task of life, at least when we believe that death is not the total dissolution of our identity but the way to its fullest revelation. Death, as Jesus speaks about it, is that moment in which

> total defeat and total victory
> are one. The cross on which
> Jesus died is the sign of this
> oneness of defeat and vic-
> tory. Jesus speaks about his
> death as being "lifted up."

The doctors said that during these last few weeks, Michael was "miraculously stable." Was *that* my miracle? We had been given a few more invaluable weeks just to be with each other, not being sure what the future might bring. Just holding on to each other was a blessing, and each day that passed fulfilled our desire for having "another day to love you." I would remind him—we have today! Today we are together, this is our moment, this is our precious now. Let us be present and ever grateful for this fleeting gift.

The day arrived for the long-awaited chemo treatment. He made it through these torturous three weeks, and we had hope, but we knew it was our last hope. It was late in the day when they began the procedure, and he was still exhausted the following day. Michael said it would be best not to have any visitors for a while, so I cancelled those scheduled. Our friends Sharon and David from Paris had just returned to the States, and they were an exception. They had been away during the whole illness and wanted to see him, and he wanted to see them. What a reunion we enjoyed, all so glad to be together again. On Monday, my good friend Barbara from Southern Pines came and stayed with Michael all day allowing me time to skip out for a couple of errands that needed attention. He was so fond of her and enjoyed the bright company. She brought dinner for us and spent the night at our house, then headed home in the morning. Things seemed stable, he was still in good spirits, and we were just waiting for that second round of chemo to kick in and make him better.

On November 6, I happily answered Michael's typical early morning text. How I loved his cheerful greetings and to read that he could not wait to see me. As I hurried on my way to the hospital, I noticed he had not sent me a reply. That was unusual. In great haste, I traversed those all-too-familiar halls of the old hospital building and navigated the elevators, finally arriving at his room where I sensed something strangely foreboding. I was delighted to see Adrienne near him along with two respiratory therapists. I asked happily, "Are you ours today?" It was always a good day with one of Michael's angels on duty.

She turned to me with, "Yes, I'm yours today," but I could tell something was wrong. She was not smiling. No one was smiling.

"What's happening?" I asked.

She replied, "He's struggling. He needs the BiPAP, and he doesn't want it."

He was moving his head side to side in distress. His eyes were closed. He could hardly respond to me. I knew he did not like the BiPAP respirator with its larger and tighter mask, but it was the one that forced air into his lungs, and if his saturation numbers were low, that was what he needed. More questions came to mind as I wrestled with this unwelcome jolt. A rush of near panic overcame me. Was I losing him? I kissed him gently and told him I was here. His eyes opened just slightly, then closed again.

I texted my pastors, and only John could come right over. Meg would be here later. I was desperately sending texts, letting all our kids know something was going on. John arrived and tried to calm me. Then he said, "Gail, put your phone down." A little stunned, I knew what he meant. He had been at enough end-of-life moments to recognize this might be one, and he did not want me to waste a single speck of whatever precious time I may have left with Michael. I am grateful for the courage he displayed to get me back in the moment.

I left the room with questions for Adrienne, and John stayed with Michael. She was right outside at her station in the wide hallway.

Terrified, I asked, "Could this be it?"

"Could be," she said, but her eyes did not meet mine.

"Should I call his kids?"

"I would," she replied, still no smile, so unlike Adrienne. "If he rallies, then great, but if he doesn't, you know you did all you could."

Back in the room, John and I watched as Michael strained and struggled to breathe. He wanted that BiPAP off, but Adrienne and the respiratory therapists agreed he might not survive the switch to the smaller, less powerful CPAP, and we should wait till his kids arrive. They were on the way, but it would take them over an hour.

As we sat on either side of his bed, I told John about Adrienne. "You will not believe this, but it was Adrienne on duty the day Mike died. I recognized her right away a few weeks ago, but she does not recognize me. With my new last name, she did not make the connection." John remembered the many hours he spent with us in the ICU while Mike was hospitalized, and he was astounded at the coincidence.

Later, John stepped out to discuss a concern with Adrienne. I sat alone with my sweet Michael and for the first time had to admit to myself that he might not make it. I can honestly say I never gave up hope till that day. But now it seemed, as fervently as we had hoped, prayed, and believed, there would be no miracle to keep him alive. I put my face up to his and kissed his forehead, the only part of his face not covered in that large, tight oxygen mask. Tears were flooding down my face as I told him I would always love him and thanked him for loving me so completely.

John did not realize I had not told Adrienne my identity, and he said something to her about the eerie coincidence that she had been the nurse on duty when my first husband, Mike, died almost six years ago. *What?* She did not know and was just as amazed.

When I spoke to her later, I began with, "John told you…"

"I always knew you looked familiar!" she exclaimed.

I apologized for not having been more open but told her I was glad she now knows. When I reminded her of my previous last name, she remembered Mike and our weeks here right away. Then I asked her, "Please… tell me…is there any chance Michael will survive?"

She lowered her eyes again and said, "I'm sorry, no. I wish I could say otherwise, but he is not going to get better. He has already survived weeks longer than expected." Then looking me straight in the eye, she proclaimed sincerely, "He didn't want to leave you!"

It was still early in the day as John and I waited for Niki and Scott to arrive. I started to notice an unusual number of visits from various doctors and even some of our favorite nurses. They were not there to treat Michael or announce any test results but instead would hug me and tell me they were so sorry and then touch his head or shoulder. I was confused. *Why were they here?* One of his favorite young doctors came up from his duties in the emergency department to sit with him for a minute. "Thanks for being my favorite patient. I'll never forget you." *Oh no, they were saying goodbye!* Clearly, the word was out that his demise was imminent. This parade of sincere but gut-wrenching dialogue was excruciating. He had made an impact on these wonderful doctors and nurses, and they were paying their respects. I was touched by this kind and generous gesture of affection. It meant so much to me, and I am sure to Michael as well if he was able to realize what was happening. I asked Adrienne for confirmation, and she nodded and said, "Gail, he touched so many lives…people are crying out here who barely knew him."

In a rare quiet moment alone with Michael, I removed the wedding ring from his finger and unhooked the cross he wore around his neck, my gift to him which he wore every day. I held them both lovingly in my hand in reluctant surrender to his impending death. Looking at his wedding ring now and kissing it gently, I could see the inscription that he chose, "How about tomorrow?" We had bet it all on having a world of tomorrows, but we had lost that bet. The endless tomorrows we longed for were dissipating before our eyes. We have our fond yesterdays, and no one can ever take that away from us. And we have today, wistful as it is. But now tragically for us, there would be no more tomorrows.

Niki and Zac arrived about 10:00 a.m., then Scott soon after. We said our goodbyes to John and thanked him. Incredulous that the moment was upon us, we held each other up as best we could. Michael opened his eyes and knew his children were near. They sat close, touched their father lovingly, and spoke to him. Soon the respiratory therapists came in to transfer him off the high-powered BiPAP and back to the smaller CPAP. With the CPAP, he could speak, which was one of his wishes for his last moments. He wanted to be able to say that he loved us and goodbye. He did not want to be intubated or otherwise restricted, so to this end, the removal of the BiPAP proceeded. We were warned that it might be more than he could tolerate to drop to the lower oxygen level without the forced air and to be prepared.

It was a terrifying few moments, but he survived the adjustment and seemed more comfortable with the less-restrictive mask. Staff and personnel continued to stop in, and we were so touched at the outpouring of sympathy and also the evidence of how he had made a small difference in their lives these past few weeks. The kind words spoken of his uplifting spirit, his nonstop positive attitude, and how he made this place a little brighter meant the world to us. And we knew it to be true. From the department head to the cleaning personnel, he was on a first-name basis. It was not enough to just say hello and be polite to someone, he wanted to know how many children they had, how long they had worked here, and where they lived.

With his training and lifelong career as a medical professional, he felt a certain kinship, but it went beyond that to his authentic self. Even in his compromised state, he did not know a stranger and reached out to see the light in the other person. Throughout his stay, he liked the curtain open so he could wave to the nurses he knew in the hallways. Sometimes when he was able, he would even move his arms and upper body as if he were dancing to enjoy a playful moment with the staff who would respond in kind. He never stopped living.

With sad trepidation, I asked Niki, Zac, and Scott to join me in the hall so we could talk privately. I needed to tell them what Adrienne had said to me earlier about his survival chances. We were all crying, and Zac said in disbelief, "You mean there is *no* chance?" Hard to say and harder yet to hear. I told them something I had learned through losing Mike. It is said those left behind need to consciously let go of their loved one at life's end. Some say that otherwise, the spirit gets stuck and stays longer in this realm, waiting for their family to let them go. As hard as it was, we all needed to send him our heartfelt messages of love and release.

I reviewed with them what Michael had called his "plan" should it come to that. Dr. Patel had discussed this with him and advised us that this mental preparation provides assurance to the patient in the final hours. If the end came, that is if his breathing kept deteriorating with no remaining options for treatment, he would be kept comfortable with increased morphine as needed. Concurrently, his oxygen supply would be decreased gradually, but he would not struggle or gasp to breathe. The end would be peaceful and with dignity. And that is what Michael wanted.

A few hours passed, and the five of us were unified in this rare moment of life and death. Michael would respond to our touch and open his eyes when prompted, but mostly, he was still. Then the unexpected happened. Without warning, the curtain by the door opened wide, and the attending doctor surrounded by six other personnel burst in the room with big smiles on their faces.

I said to Michael, "Wake up! Look who's here!" and his beautiful eyes opened. He rallied, nodded, and lifted his head just a bit.

From behind his back, the doctor pulled out a glass mason jar with a handle, filled with beer, and extended it, saying, "Cheers!"

Everyone knew Michael would predictably end his conversations with the hospital team promising, "When I get out of here, we're gonna meet up for a Blue Moon with an orange!" So, they honored him today—with a cold Blue Moon, a big chunk of orange, and a straw. They handed me the jar, and I held it as he had a sip.

They clapped and declared, "A toast to Michael!" as he mouthed the words *thank you* with his hands in prayer position.

We resumed the bedside watch, sensing it would be soon. Quiet observation of the sacred moment mixed with disbelief and tears permeated our time and space. It was midafternoon, and we requested no more visitors, not even doctors. Adrienne was attentive to his every need, and ours, answering our nervous questions with patience and grace. Michael's breathing became somewhat irregular, and she increased the morphine. Some adjustment was made to the respirator; then, she turned the wall-mounted monitor away from us so we would not see the declining numbers and be alarmed or distracted. Adrienne left us alone with him and pulled the curtain shut. His breathing continued to slow, and we watched the cadence fluctuate. This sweet man—husband, father, and father-in-law—was crossing over into another realm. He was leaving us. We stayed close, touching him, loving him, sensing the mystery and majesty of this moment. An eerie stillness surrounded us. A few minutes later, Adrienne entered the room and announced what we already knew, "He has passed."

Hugs and tears ensued as we tried to process what had just happened. Adrienne removed the CPAP, and we could kiss his beautiful face without the interference of the mask and the plastic tubing. At last, he was no longer tethered to machines and monitors. We stood around his bed holding hands and encircling him with our love as I offered up a prayer of thanks for the gift of his life to each of us and for all his pure goodness. I looked up to the ceiling once again, as I had done almost six years ago in a similar room just down the hall, looking for those angels who came to carry our beloved up to heaven.

We all took time for a private moment to say our goodbyes as we consoled each other in our communal loss and pain. Later when emotions permitted, we talked about the service. It would be held at our Presbyterian church where Michael and I were members, in downtown Chapel Hill. Niki would write the obituary, and Scott would deliver a eulogy.

We lingered as we comforted each other; then, we texted and called family members and close friends with the sad news. Adrienne brought us a box so we could remove the dozens of greeting cards taped all over the room and take them home. Later, she brought a cart to load up remaining items and take down to the parking lot. It became time to go, and one by one, we embraced him and said our final farewell while still in the presence of his earthly shell. Before leaving the room, we stood around our beloved Michael for that last sacred moment as he lay there motionless, his head turned to the side. It was so hard to leave him in that room, and as I walked out, I had to turn back and look one more time. Adrienne walked with us all the way to my car, which had been delivered from valet parking. They asked if I would be okay, and I told them Amy was on her way to be with me. She would bring dinner and spend the night. We hugged and turned to go home. He was gone. *Oh Lord, how could it be?*

Planning for the memorial service went smoothly under Meg's skilled guidance. All three pastors would participate as had been the case with Mike. Meg and Jarrett were relatively new to us, but my longtime friend and pastor John would hold my hand once again as I said goodbye to another husband. The next day, Meg met with all of us around our dining room table as we agreed upon a date and planned the details of the service. She patiently listened to all our remembrances of this fine man and masterfully wove our loving comments into her delivery for the service of witness to the resurrection.

At the funeral home the next day, with my sister, Niki, Zac, and Scott, we dealt with the necessary decisions and paperwork for his cremation. I ordered prayer cards to be distributed at the service and chose the scripture to be printed on the back along with his name and dates, "In loving memory." It would be Romans 8:38–39, the same verses read to us by the doctor and minister just a few days ago. The message repeated in my head, that nothing shall be able to separate us from the love of God, no nothing.

We were thrilled to learn that his brother Larry would attend the funeral! Larry and his son Zachery would make the drive from Canada and demonstrate in person his love and forgiveness. Niki worked hard and did a beautiful job writing the heart-wrenching obituary. It was published online just in time to get the word out about the service. In it, she said, "Michael will be remembered by many for his contagious smile, his generosity, sense of humor, kindness, and zest for life. He always made those around him feel loved and special. His compassion and way of living life to its fullest was inspiring." We gathered multiple photos and mementos for the remembrance table at the reception. His hockey jersey and ice skates, along with a special baseball, a Canadian flag, the blinking Eiffel Tower, and so much more painted a vivid snapshot of his remarkable life.

Family on both sides along with several of our closest couple friends gathered in the church's Memorial Garden before the service to scatter his ashes. We were grateful for a beautiful day—warm for November with lots of sun. Meg's beautiful words and prayers ended with: "In the sure and certain hope of resurrection to eternal life, through our Lord Jesus Christ we commend to almighty God, our brother Michael, and we commit his body to the ground, earth to earth, ashes to ashes, dust to dust." Now the ashes of my two husbands would mingle here forever in this sacred place.

We waited in the parlor while friends and family arrived at the church to pay their respects. Honored at the large turnout, we knew it was a testament to his life well lived.

When it was time, we processed in from the back of the sanctuary and sat in the first few rows, which had been reserved. Meg began with, "A remarkable presence is gone from our midst. And though it is painful, it is good that we are here. For we gather to celebrate the life of God's beloved child, Michael Francis Lefaive."

Later in the service, Scott delivered a moving tribute with his words of remembrance. He said, "He taught us to always be present in the moment, to recognize that transgressions from our past did not identify us, and that any future was in our hands, to mold it into any form we wished."

Pastor John who had been with my family and me through so much offered a reflection on *radiance*: God's *radiance* and Michael's radiance. He said, "Though this is certainly a time that deep sadness has pitched a tent in our lives, may she have co-companions of certainty and joy so that we all are reminded of a light that is never consumed by the darkness of our despair. So, shine on, O Light of the world, into this space, into our hearts, Your radiance!"

After the service, the fellowship hall was filled with many of the over two hundred well-wishers for the reception. A long center table, blanketed with fresh white tablecloths and colorful fall floral arrangements, bore plate after plate of sandwiches, sweets, and other refreshments donated from our church friends. Tracy, the cake lady who had made our glorious wedding cake and also the three-tiered beauty for the Garden Club Picnic, had dropped off a custom cake for us with the frosting swirled up magnificently to represent a giant rose, the symbol of love. The remembrance table was crowded as groups of people shifted up and down to get a little closer glimpse into the kind soul we came to honor and remember that day.

Niki, Zac, Scott, and I stood together in a back section of the large open hall to receive the guests. The queue took shape and kept growing. Good friends brought us water to sip and fresh tissues to replace our wet ones as we stood there being lifted up by so many who came to offer their condolences. It took nearly an hour to greet those standing patiently in that long line of love, and it just about took our last shred of strength. Hugs, hugs, and more hugs were warmly exchanged. Kind words, offers to help us cope, and reassurances of prayers for his grieving family abundantly comforted us like warm sunshine after a rain, our *après la pluie* of the heart. Friends and coworkers from both sides of the family were present, and Larry was able to see in person this outpouring of love for his brother and our communal sadness at this great loss.

Then came a special moment as we recognized the next group in line. Michael's angels were here! Adrienne, Christine, Sophie, Beth, Caille, and Susan all looked different with their hair done, some makeup on, and in street clothes instead of hospital scrubs and ponytails, but we quickly recognized these favorite nurses from the ICU. We were all so touched to see them, these smart, remarkable young women who gave extra special loving care to Michael all these weeks. We took a picture as they stood arm in arm, sensing their presence was something of an honor, rare and unexpected. Adrienne spoke up as a few others circled around. Her words, sincere and poignant, rang out, "We don't do this." She shook her head and continued vehemently, "We don't come to the funeral. We are trained not to get attached, but he ruined us on that. He broke all the rules, then we did too." There they were—so talented, beautiful, and giving up their day off to pay homage to this extraordinary patient who captured their hearts and to make sure we knew why they were here.

My daughters and his children, some out-of-town friends and lots of extended family came back to our house after the service so we could continue our visit. We brought home all the lavish flowers that had been sent to the church and the various items from the remembrance table. So strange—it was like a party with good food, smiling people taking photos, and pleasant conversation. But then again, it was not like any party anyone really ever wants to attend.

I was so happy to show Larry around so he could picture Michael at our home and see his office. While we walked the garden, I told him and Zachery how much Michael loved helping me care for it and pointed out various contributions he had made in our short time here. As they were leaving, we came upon the framed photo of the toddlers on the piano stool, which had been displayed on the remembrance table. I handed it to Larry. "Here, this should be with you now."

This extraordinary day was coming to an end. It was a meaningful sendoff for a very special man who touched so many lives. And oh, how he had touched my life! Emotions collided and filled my heart as I thought how lucky I was to have had such special time with him and how cheated I felt that he was taken from me so soon. It had been the worst nightmare, but it was finally over—or was it? Perhaps my nightmare was just beginning…

9

Jailhouse Blues

I sat down at the
lunch counter
in the True Story Café
and looked at the menu.
I was so hungry.
I had not ordered yet,
but I was served
Today's Special,
a Grief Sandwich.
It was a couple of good years
between two missing
Michaels.
It made me sick.

*N*ot again. Oh, please Lord, not again.
    Where am I? Confused, as if waking up
from a dream—or worse yet, a nightmare—I

see myself standing alone in a brick courtyard garden formed by exterior walls of my church building. Filled with blooming seasonal treasures, it is home to flowering trees, shrubs, perennials, and a multitude of colorful bulbs. I see delicate powder blue forget-me-nots dancing around the edges proclaiming their heartfelt entreaty. I cringe at the reminder. My soul begs, "Please, not again!"

I wander beneath a wisteria-covered arbor providing shade and hear the rhythmic music of trickling water from a nearby fountain that fills the air. In the center of the arbor floor, a Celtic cross has been carved into a stone medallion. Around it, these precious words whisper, "Peace I leave with you. My peace I give to you" (John 14:27 RSV).

Nearby, a wide mulched area bares itself to become the sacred space where the cremated ashes of loved ones are buried or scattered. Above that hallowed ground, a granite slab mounted on the brick façade records the details of those dear ones here interred. I take a deep breath. Through moist eyes, I search the stone panels for the names, the names of my two husbands lost within six years of each other.

Despair and sorrow overcome me. I can barely hear the quiet voice inside promising me that I will survive. It is there, if only a faint whisper. Even in my dream state, I can tell this dark place is all too familiar, a place I never wanted to be again. Grief is a place in my heart I do not wish to linger, but this harsh reality has brought me back in time.

I feel confined, banished—imprisoned in some cruel, emotional dungeon that holds me against my will. "I've done nothing wrong! I don't belong here!" I cry. But there is no one to hear my pleas. There is no one to bail me out. I wake up to a solitary confinement worse than anything imaginable. Isolation and seclusion once again dominate my world. These two somber sisters co-conspire to shepherd me until I banish them. If I allow it, I will seek and find a path to contemplation, which offers a way out.

Through genuine deliberation, we can discover truth and invite transformation. With these worthy goals, we discern how to escape the worst. We cannot flee grief itself, but with awareness and openness to growth, we can minimize some of the trauma and damage that often occurs. This time, I will—I must—cope better. I now know we have choices and meaningful ways to help us endure.

The chilly air seeping in through my bedroom window snaps me out of my trance.

I become aware of just standing still, gazing aimlessly out at nothing. That nothingness transports me back and forth between my deepest, darkest thoughts and fleeting periods of lucidity. I cringe at the thought of going back to that pernicious place where I suffered, literally, for years. I think to myself, *I will not, I cannot go back to that noxious captivity.* Yet here I am once again facing the reality of a terrible loss and the season of sorrow dragging along behind me like a ball and chain. Here I am, once again facing what feels like an extended sentence to grief prison. Like some monster that morphed out of a wretched condemnation, it grew legs and chased me in the night. Is there no balm in Gilead? Has some cosmic debt come due? Has some forgotten penance been imposed?

Have I *not* suffered enough at losing this dear man and all our tomorrows without further retribution? I cannot reconcile this nefarious iniquity in my mind, but I know one thing for certain: I am *not* going back to *grief prison*.

Pastor Bob sent me this poem by Jan Richardson after Mike's death six years ago. I read the poignant words again now with even greater insight into the truth of which it speaks so eloquently.

BLESSING FOR THE BROKENHEARTED

There is no remedy for love but to love more.
—Henry David Thoreau

Let us agree
for now
that we will not say
the breaking
makes us stronger
or that it is better
to have this pain
than to have done
without this love.

Gail Norwood

Let us promise
we will not
tell ourselves
time will heal
the wound
when every day
our waking
opens it anew.

Perhaps for now
it can be enough
to simply marvel
at the mystery
of how a heart
so broken
can go on beating,
as if it were made
for precisely this—

as if it knows
the only cure for love
is more of it,

as if it sees
the heart's sole remedy
for breaking
is to love still,

as if it trusts
that its own
persistent pulse
is the rhythm
of a blessing
we cannot
begin to fathom
but will save us
nonetheless.

Almost right away after losing Michael, I vowed to respond differently than I had after losing Mike. I had the benefit of my earlier experience to lean on for starters. What I absorbed during the first unbearable bereavement helped me learn the basics of grief. I learned a lot in Grief 101—in fact, I aced it. I learned that I must now don whatever survival equipment available to buoy my soul and psyche as I once again struggle to stay afloat amid the raging waters. I learned that I must now make a conscious effort to fortify myself with whatever means available to avoid experiencing the agonizing darkness again. I learned about choices. Unlike after my first tragic loss, I felt stronger, more confident, and at least somewhat in control.

Much of my confidence and strength came from my recent discovery of the concept of *good grief.* Aside from Charlie Brown, I first heard the term used in the context of healing in a sermon one Sunday. That happened to be my first time back to church since losing Michael. This was months earlier than I attended services after Mike died, and it was part of my determination not to repeat my prior mistakes. Our hometown Presbyterian church had recently welcomed a dynamic young couple to lead us as co-pastors after the retirement of our beloved senior pastor Bob. Meg, a smart, savvy forty-something woman soon revealed herself to be an accomplished speaker, her sermons insightful and authentic. She and her husband, Jarrett, equally impressive from the pulpit, had quickly infused our congregation with powerful energy drawn from their youth, wisdom, and fresh approach. The last time I had seen them was when they presided over a genuinely meaningful and poignant memorial service for Michael, for which I would be forever grateful.

It felt good to be in that beautiful sanctuary again even though predictably I needed lots of tissues. Only a couple of months earlier, I had been there to say goodbye to Michael amid a great uplifting from so many loved ones. As Meg began to speak that Sunday, she told the congregation something a friend of hers had said about grieving. Her friend was a mentor in ministry to her, and while they were helping a family tend to funeral planning, he prayed with them for a *good grief*. She said, "It was a plea that this family's grief be good, healthy, and productive. That they would feel the feelings as they came up rather than smooshing them down, that they would have friends with whom they did not have to pretend everything was fine. He sincerely wanted their grief to be good." As I hugged Meg at the door on my way out of church, I expressed my appreciation for those comments that felt so personal, as if she were talking just to me. She admitted she thought of me as she wrote those words on *good grief*, and it meant even more.

I would strive to make *good grief* my goal, a grief that was good, healthy, and productive. At this point, I was not sure exactly what that meant, but I had a strong, positive feeling about it. I would devote myself to finding out what would make it good and make it my own. It clearly begins with the power of suggestion—the mere suggestion of *good grief* from Meg was all I needed to even consider such a thing was possible. Her words gave me permission to look for the good in grief. Just what I needed to hear; these wise powerful words set me in a new direction.

I could look back now and see that the years after losing Mike were darkness and despair personified. I could barely speak of my sorrow and loneliness then, finding true healing slow and burdensome. One step forward, two steps back. Years passed. Any lessons I learned were more after the fact than in the moment. I was too numb, too scared, too stuck in the muck. When I first heard this quote by Bohemian Austrian poet Rilke, I was stunned and immediately understood its significance.

How we squander
our hours of pain.

Waste, recklessness, foolishness—these are words that speak of squander. Yes, I had wasted the hour of my pain after losing Mike. I squandered it shamelessly. I wasted months and years of my life in a prolonged grief that could have and *should have* been less traumatic. I wasted listening for, then hearing the truths I was supposed to be learning. I wasted visits and comfort offered by friends and family by shutting them out. I squandered the opportunities it offered me to grow, choosing to be a victim of my grief instead. I had squandered precious days of my life in a self-imposed, ill-directed, and negative expression of my sorrow. I now know not to squander this painful time but see instead the embedded opportunities it offers.

In contrast, the months after losing Michael were more about enlightenment. Of course, I was overwhelmed with many of the same excruciating emotions I had suffered before, but I also knew from the very start that I was not going to go through that hell again, and that somehow, I had to protect myself from the very real potential damage. To do so, I spent endless hours reading, studying, and in prayer as if I had entered my own personal *grief seminary*. For starters, I longed to extinguish the need to understand this unimaginable loss, but what I came to know instead is that there is just no answer. Mysteries and tragedies of life that befall us are not accountable to anyone here on earth. These early months in my own seminary and meditation served me well. I was set on a different path: one paved with messages of truths that would allow me to escape another immurement in grief prison.

The lessons came, one after the other. Perhaps I was more open to them because I so wanted this hurt to go away. *Just heal me and let me leave this place of darkness*, I prayed. In fact, it felt more like a shield, a form of self-preservation to be open to a new way of thinking. I can say with some certainty that instead of speaking about sorrow and loneliness, I now speak of a deeper awareness the role loss and disappointment play in each of our lives. When our tears dry enough for us to see clearly, we can choose to embrace new truths that are now apparent.

The too familiar shock and numbness of enduring the holidays was glaring. It was insult to injury to witness the rest of the world proceed with the traditional celebrations. Did they not all know my world was over? The powerful undertow of a second grief was taking hold.

Before I knew it, Thanksgiving arrived, and I spent the day and night at Amy's house where a large group of friends and family gathered to celebrate the day. My sister, Janine, was there and Don's extended family. Mary Evelyn and Andy had come from Georgia, and all four grandchildren laughing and playing together provided much needed levity. Six-year-old Isaac secretly rearranged the sixteen place cards at the fully decorated dining table, which Amy had carefully placed earlier. She discovered this just in time, and his mischievous prank was a delightful diversion from the heavier conversation. I did not feel like being in a room full of people, but I did not want to be alone on Thanksgiving either. I had not seen some of the guests since

Michael's passing, and they kindly expressed their condolences, which was so painful to endure in that public setting. But of course, I did not expect them to say nothing, and of course, they did not expect me *not* to cry.

I was grateful to have my wonderful family around me, especially both my daughters, but I was missing Michael terribly, and the wound was still too new. For Christmas, I escaped to my sister's home in Williamsburg. There we enjoyed the celebrated colonial holiday decorations, and on a sunny Christmas morning, we attended services at historic Bruton Parish Church where I did not know anyone, and that felt good. Back home in Chapel Hill, it was just as it had been after Mike died—no evidence of any holiday. No wreath, no tree, no cookie baking, no Christmas cards, no candles, no carols on the piano...no Michael.

I did not feel like it, but I had to make myself deal with closing Michael's accounts and managing the endless details of his estate. Having to do this in my weak condition was torturous. Misery upon grief. Another pressing task was to gather up all his things—his personal items—and make them available to Niki and Scott. That special baseball he had kept all these years, his signed hockey jerseys, his skates, old photos from Canada, and lots of his sweaters and clothes crowded the top of my dining room table, theirs for the taking. It was hard on them to go through these items so familiar and nostalgic, but they did so with generosity and graciousness to the feelings of the other. They loaded their cars, and off they went, taking with them most of the evidence that Michael had ever lived here. In truth, I did not really care because I did not want his *things*, I wanted him, but he was gone. The two personal treasures that were mine—his wedding ring and the cross he wore around his neck—were kept in a little heart-shaped dish by our bed that bore the words "I love us."

I put away most of our framed photos that were displayed all over the house. It was just too painful to look at them and be reminded of happier times. The group family picture taken at our wedding printed on a large canvas had to go. I could not walk past it each day. A few favorite photos remained in my office, but the rest were gathered in a special place where I kept other things he had given me or we had received as wedding gifts. The few months that we shared were so glorious, and the pictures told the tale of our travels and our growing love. I was reminded of a quote Michael used to say to me before we knew our time together would be so brief, "A happy marriage is a long conversation which always seems too short" (Andre Maurois).

Another tedious chore involved changing my name back to Norwood. I had been a Norwood for forty-seven years and was only a Lefaive for just over six months. Michael used to say to me with a smile and satisfaction, "You finally have a French name!" and I did delight in the name Lefaive as he did. But changing back to Norwood is just what felt right to me. I did not want to be a *Lefaive* without my Lefaive.

The aloneness was setting in, and I despised it. Solitary confinement had once again been imposed. I had felt it strongly after losing Mike. Aloneness is uniquely different from loneliness. I was again on my own. I was alone. Loneliness is a sadness, an emotional response to aloneness. That loneliness would almost certainly come as I progressed through the coming maze of sentiments, but for now, what I noticed was the stark solitariness. Michael and I had shared such a closeness, such intimacy that to acknowledge the absence of our togetherness was nothing short of agonizing. He was such a positive and vibrant presence in my every day, and now that place he occupied was empty. An empty place next to me as I sat on the deck in the evening, an empty place next to me as I had morning coffee, an empty place next to me in bed each night—and all night. I know I was blessed to have an extensive support system from family and friends, but as anyone who has been through this kind of loss can tell you, family and friends cannot fill the void of losing a spouse or a lover, and for me, he was both.

My mind raced back to all the messages and good wishes in the engagement and wedding cards, touting how life is meant to be shared, and experiences are always better with two. When I heard "God created us for companionship" in a wedding ceremony, it cut like a razor-sharp sting. How does any of this make sense if some of us—many of us—are alone? I do not have any answer and can barely tolerate the question. But aloneness and struggling with its meaning and purpose have been for me a big part of coming to peace with my tragedy.

The dreaded holidays were now past, and just as before after losing Mike, I detected a *bleak midwinter* setting in. It was January, and a flurry of memories of the first grief were flashing before me as I resisted their imminent suggestions. I knew my first loss had been complicated and grueling, and I did not want to endure that pain again. Did I have any choice in the matter? Could I have a say in this, or was it a certain cruel destiny?

I recognized a revelation emerging about how I could take a different path. I held tight to that promise and did not let it go. I was consumed with thoughts of how I did not want to make myself sick again or stay in as a recluse for too long or keep my friends and supporters at bay as I had done before. I started to contemplate thoughts of how I had handled my first grief and how much

I did not want a repeat performance. What could I do differently this time? I had chosen to pursue *good grief,* and now I must make it happen. Hope and comfort waited patiently from afar as I gently turned toward them.

It honestly felt like another prison sentence was being handed down after Michael's death, and I started to sense the walls closing in around me. I did not want to go there. I remembered the barren days that overshadowed three and a half years spent in the *dark side*, and it was unfathomable that I should repeat it in any way. Was my being down and out somehow fulfilling the expectations of society and traditional grief therapy? As I pondered the question, I found myself aimlessly staring out the window again. Just staring and thinking and hoping for an answer, a new way out of this precipitous mandate.

In spite of my emotional intention and determination to heal in a healthier way, I realized suddenly that I had already started repeating my regrettable habits from round one. I had been completely staying by myself and not seeing friends or hardly talking to them on the phone. No church, no meetings, no Bible study, no shopping, no visitors. And oh the tears, the tears that could be measured in the rain gauge. It was tears and tissues all day; tears and mascara-stained sheets all night.

I caught myself and said, *Stop! Don't do this again!* I called my sister, Janine. I told her how I hated being thought of as the pitiful widow again, a role I despised. I knew people meant well, but when they called or e-mailed to "check on me," it felt odd and uncomfortable. I had always been the person who checked on others, not the person being checked on, and it was creepy. I did not want to be that needy person who needed to be checked on, who *needed* help.

She barked right back the best advice ever, "If you do not want people to worry about you and think of you as a pitiful widow, then get out of the house, slap a smile on your face, and let people know you are doing okay!!" That was just the kick I needed to shake out of this new self-imposed cocoon. I knew she was right.

It was time to have a talk with myself. Yes, this happened to me, and it was awful, but I will not be a victim. And no more pity party! I have control over that. *We* have control over that. We either think of ourselves as mistreated victims or not. It is a choice. That's right—it was not fair, we do not understand why, and it was not supposed to be this way, but in the end, life happens. We all suffer, but we may not always suffer well.

More than a reminder of the Johnny Cash song title from the 1950s, the phrase "Walk the Line" has a particular meaning in this conversation. Prisons and jails in the early twentieth century had lines or paths on the floor or grounds to keep the prisoners in order as they lined up for exercise in the yard or formed a queue to change locations in the *big house*. The armed guards would shout the order, and compliance was expected. In the prison yard, edged with tall barbed-wire-laced fences, the dirt path circles around in infamy. The prisoners must walk the line over and over until the allotted time outside has passed.

As we "do our time" in grief, it sometimes feels as if we are "walking the line." Someone or something has told us to get in line and stay there. The content from a book, a well-meaning friend, or some random subliminal societal message has been heard, and we comply. The authoritative mandate is so strong, we accept it and do as we are told. Sometimes it can feel like we are just walking in circles even though we know we are looking for healing and new life. Just walk. Just keep walking, we are told. Walking in circles and not going anywhere. Walking in circles and not getting anywhere. But when it is time, my fellow jailbirds, then we break out—escape—and get out of line. We get off the painted line on the cement, and we choose our own path.

This is where a choice comes in, if we know we have one. If we are not bound by societal mandates or subliminal messages, we can foster a keen awareness of when we do and do not have a choice. Awareness is one of the keys that opens the lock of our jail cell—feel the freedom! Do not listen to the whispers, the cautions, the greeting cards that mean well. Or if you must ingest the messages because it is hard to avoid them, then see them for what they are: options, not mandates. Own it. Remember always, we have choices.

Encouraged that I could do things differently, I slowly started to reach out to friends and have them over for a chat and a cup of tea. I clearly proclaimed that things were not going to be like last time, and I was going to be okay. Sarah called, and I excitedly gave her my news and told her of my intentions for this new healing. I had not spoken with her in a few weeks, and she said she could hear the exhilaration in my voice for my newfound strength. Hearing her say that felt good and reinforced my determination to hold steady. I would tell Barbara, Sharon, Hilda, and other friends how strongly I felt about minimizing the damage and how I intended to move forward.

I was developing a plan. I wanted to abbreviate my pain, to abbreviate the process. Some offered support and favor while a few others expressed doubt that I could "buck the system." I understood the disparity of reactions because I myself had sampled them all.

A few more grief books were given to me. Not nearly as many as before, and I had long since given away the earlier ones, passing them along to others who sadly had joined this widow or widower club of which no one wants to be a member. I read them with a different perspective, taking into account all I had been through and now incorporating my newfound enlightenment. I found some parts of them very helpful and uplifting and other parts downright offensive. Now that I was able to discern the negative innuendos that can be tacked on to well-meaning grief advice, they stood out to me loud and clear.

My expanded reading included the discovery of an uplifting concept that proved to be a solid inspiration. It declared there is always a blue sky even if sometimes clouds obscure it. The blue sky has not changed or disappeared, but it is not currently visible. In this hour of sadness, I proclaim that I am the blue sky behind the temporary clouds of grief that are just passing by. The *real* me, the me that had to endure losing Mike and the life we had, then endure losing Michael and the future we had, was still there just as before. The real me who is genuinely optimistic and happy, the real me who is joyful and thankful, the real me who does not want to be pitied—that real me is waiting patiently behind the clouds and believing they will one day move on. The *real* me is there and has not changed, still boldly blue and still waiting with a glimmer of hope for what is just beyond.

I was shaken out of my contemplation by a knock at the door. I did not feel like company, and I was not prone to answer. I peeked out the window to see who was there. It was the warden from grief prison! I held my breath.

Knock, knock, knock, it repeated.

"Go away!" I shouted.

Knock, knock, knock. The faceless uniformed figure had a paper rolled up in his hand, and he wielded it as if it were some kind of emotional truncheon. The knocking continued. Did he have a subpoena?

"Go away!" I demanded.

"It's time for you to come back," he said threateningly.

"I will *not* come back," I declared. "*Never.* You have no power over me. I am no longer at your mercy."

Knock, knock, knock.

I will not let him in. The door and the lock are strong and will protect me. The truths I have learned about grief and how to survive are strong and will protect me. I stand defiantly as I watch him from the window. The knocking finally ends, but he pauses on the stoop. He returns his paper baton to his inside coat pocket. With a sigh, he turns to leave.

"I'll be back," he groans ominously. As he walks away, I affirm to myself, *I will not be bullied.* I will not return to grief prison. I will not be at his mercy again. This is my choice, and I have made it.

Yes, I could feel it happening. I had turned a corner. The enlightenment I had experienced in these past few months had shored me up against the emotional onslaught. I felt stronger. I was learning the lessons and gaining a deeper understanding as my time in grief seminary progressed. The reading, the studying, the prayer all continued daily and even accelerated as I began to feel the fortitude filling me up. I was not going back to grief prison, and I had solidly discovered my choices in how I would move forward.

My life lessons and study reinforced the truth that disappointments are part of life, and there was no promise that everything would be fair. Or that *anything* would be fair. A certain amount of suffering is not unusual in the human condition, and while we cannot control it or understand it, we can try to accept it and grow. We have the opportunity to learn whatever spiritual lessons are presented from any experience. Apparently, there are a lot of lessons to be learned. One we are reminded of repeatedly is the importance of gratitude, no matter what. The message seems to be that it is through life's disappointments and losses that we are invited to focus on that for which we are grateful, find and experience our higher self, and discover a closer relationship with our Creator and Savior.

Winter turned to spring reminding me of a favorite Kahlil Gibran quote I first heard as a young woman, "If winter should say, 'spring is in my heart,' who would believe winter?" In winter, we cannot even picture in our minds the glorious landscape of spring about to erupt, but we know in our hearts it is coming. In the winter of our grief, our bleak midwinter, we cannot help question if joy and happiness will ever be ours again, when all along deep down, we know it is also coming, just as surely as spring.

Long hours in the garden sharpened my awareness of the connection between nature and God. I made an effort to keep up with routine chores better than I had six years ago, now more aware of the consequences. My bluebirds would not be neglected again; I happily cleaned and readied their boxes in time for the new breeding season. Spring was coming, and bluebird land was full of activity. I set up a garden chair within viewing distance and bid them good morning each day. Sometimes they would detect my presence and appear at their small, round opening as if to return my early greeting. Sipping my coffee and saying my daily prayers, I sat watchfully and peacefully as they entertained me with their graceful acts of love.

My backyard paradise had proven to be faithful and forgiving. As spring unfolded, I witnessed my favorite shrubs and flowers budding, then blooming right on schedule. To welcome them again lifted my spirits, bursting out of dormancy as hope personified. For the first time ever, I thought of our heavenly Father as I felt the warm sunshine on my skin. Increased prayer and meditation resulted in a renewed closeness with God, especially when immersed in the garden. The bright warm sun almost felt like He was smiling down at me. I lifted my grateful eyes and face to heaven, basking in the consoling radiance, and lovingly smiled right back at Him.

I was feeling better, and more than that, I was much better than I had been only six months after losing Mike. Trying to make each day as joyful and meaningful as I could, I embarked upon a soulful journey of prayer and reflection as I practiced smiling, choosing happiness now, and looking to God for comfort and direction. I sighed relief to compare the previous dark times and discover my currently improved situation. Of course, the circumstances had been so different, but just because my time with Michael had been shorter does not correlate with the amount of sadness and loss I processed. These two men that I loved were different, our love and lives together were different, and dealing with their losses was different.

As dissimilar as they were, the coincidental similarities that existed were hard to believe. Both Mike age sixty-nine, and Michael age seventy, shared the same first name and married the same woman. They were both admitted into the same intensive care unit at UNC Memorial Hospital in October. They would both die there in November, one after thirty-seven days and the other after forty days. Both had a lung disease, and both were initially diagnosed with pneumonia. Neither could breathe on his own. The same nurse, Adrienne, was on duty the day they each died and pronounced to the family, "He has passed." The cremated remains of both men were scattered in the courtyard Memorial Garden at University Presbyterian Church in Chapel Hill, North Carolina. Their names were carved in stone on the same granite panel above the sacred plot. The same distinct autumnal weather was the familiar backdrop, with shorter days, changing leaves, and dropping temperatures. Slow, painful holidays followed each death, leading into a January bleak midwinter heralding two very different seasons of grief for their widow.

But their widow was going to survive. I had not been in the slammer, but I had done my time. I had grown leaps and bounds since last fall, and I knew I was stronger. Still emotional when I talked about Michael, I remembered what my friend Hilda told me on a visit where I broke down. "Respect your tears," she advised. "They are there for a purpose." I did not doubt that, but I was so tired of crying. I was finding my balance. I was also leaps and bounds ahead of round one being so much more at peace by summertime. This was working, and I felt empowered by my progress.

Summer quietly passed; then unbelievably, it was fall again, reopening the wounds of two unspeakable autumns still fresh in my mind. I was closing in on the first anniversary of Michael's death. How I dreaded the mournful reminder. I was sentenced to another term in grief prison, but I stood my ground and refused to go. I learned some valuable lessons that helped direct my path and protected myself with all the spiritual armor I could amass. It was not easy, and still the tears persisted, so uninvited and sudden. The warden came by a few more times, but I told him to go away and refused to open the door. He could not make me come back, and he knew it. I had escaped. I was free—free to believe in forced awakenings, free to make my own choices, and free to believe in a new tomorrow.

We can turn our *jailhouse blues* into our *jailhouse rock*. We can overcome external influences that do not work for us. We can reject suggestions of how we *should* be responding to our pain that do not fit. We can look for ways to strengthen our spiritual muscles and to reap the benefits of a new closeness with our Maker. We can chase away this bleak midwinter, always trusting that spring is in its heart. With renewed courage, let us grab those lingering blues and turn them in to a bright new song that rocks your world back to life!

10

Grief Debrief

In the prison of your soul
Fear and grief may
take control.
Oppressive as they
both may be
Allow the truth to set you free.

—By the Author

*M*ike is gone. Michael is gone. The trinity of my body, mind, and soul survived this great loss, and my *light* was not overcome by the darkness. I remain with the living for now, changed and enlightened. Graduating with flying colors from my own personal crash course at grief seminary, I earned a degree in *death and rebirth, loss and renewal,* proclaiming a firm resolve to embrace life with a determination to live again. Fear and grief had been in control and kept me in prison far too long. They each had such power and darkness that when combined, the force they created was the very definition of oppressive. But there was something they could not dominate. Truth was even stronger and ever present. Truth was there tripudiating amid a joyful flutter of angel wings. Truth was the heavenly beacon of light that showed me a new way of thinking, a new awareness, and a path to escape to freedom.

Grief seminary is most accommodating. There are no applications or entrance fees. The only prerequisite is your desire to attend and to assimilate the empowering curriculum. Each semester is as long or short as you wish. There is only one sacred entry on the booklist of required reading, and you probably already own a copy. You enroll in classes based on your needs and experience. My personal course load included various subjects, each one bringing the new thought, perspective, or idea I most needed to learn. Instead of a diploma, upon completion, you will be presented with a stack of "Get Out of Jail Free" cards, which will come in very handy indeed!

Thin Places

*Where the veil
that separates
heaven and earth is lifted.*

A few months after I lost Michael, I was corresponding with my friend and pastor, John. Something I mentioned about how I wanted to survive this grief with less personal damage than before prompted him to remark, "Gail, I have no doubt that the Lord has taken you into what the Celtic Christians called a *thin place* in your life." I was unfamiliar with the phrase, but I found this ancient saying, passed down for centuries:

> Heaven and earth are only three feet apart but in the thin places that distance is even shorter. A thin place is where the veil that separates heaven and earth is lifted and one is able to glimpse the glory of God.

Thin places can be both physical locations and a state of mind. Some detect the thin veil between heaven and earth, between man and God—in a sacred place. Walking with the pilgrims on the Camino de Santiago in Spain is said to be such a setting or standing in awe at the Grand Canyon in Arizona. Entering a magnificent centuries-old cathedral in Europe can beckon the experience. Climbing the rocky peaks of Croagh Patrick in Ireland would surely qualify. Or consider the chapel in Chimayo, New Mexico, known for healing miracles, also called the Lourdes of America. Something as routine as pausing in your own garden, standing near a bubbling stream in the mountains, or the moment you first look into the eyes of your newborn child can transport you there. Our physical senses are so heightened in these sterling moments that perhaps we are allowed to move past our basic human perceptions to a deeper understanding.

When two separate worlds or entities become closer than usual, that is a thin place. When the world of subconscious dreaming drifts into a conscious awakening, for just the most fleeting moment we are between the two, in neither one nor the other. Unable to fully discern what is happening, something deep within each of us must recognize and interpret the wonder. Where one thing ends, another begins, and they just ever so slightly brush up against each other. It is this ineffable in-betweenness that provides such a mysterious and blessed state. Caught up in the mesmerizing stillness of the divine moment, we enter a realm of mystifying grace.

So what did John mean when he said I was in a thin place? Surely when I stood at the bedsides of Mike and Michael as they crossed the threshold to the next world, that was a thin place. The resulting trauma of their losses brought me closer to God as I learned the associated lessons. My withdrawal from the world as I knew it allowed me to focus and concentrate on a new set of priorities. I slowed down enough to understand the nurturing value of meditation and contemplation. I turned to God for guidance and discernment. This thin place was one of wonder and awe, taking me to a new level of spiritual growth as the veil was lifted and I "glimpsed the glory of God."

Without question, I did feel closer to God, a closeness that was not just in prayer but one that permeated each day. These bittersweet weeks and months punctuated with contemplation and solitude urged me to nurture my soul. As the saying goes, "Change is inevitable, growth is optional," and I chose to grow. I sensed a sacred invitation to draw near, and I accepted. I did not *choose* to be in this place, but finding myself here, I listened to my heart and to the gentle voice that whispered inside. I wanted to do a healthier job of grieving than before, and increasingly, I felt I was on the right path.

Liminal Space

Betwixt and Between

Richard Rohr is a globally recognized ecumenical teacher, best-selling author, and a Franciscan priest of the New Mexico Province. He is the founder of the Center for Action and Contemplation (CAC) in Albuquerque, New Mexico. Father Richard's teaching is grounded in the Franciscan alternative orthodoxy, and his daily e-mail meditations have been part of my mornings for many years. He offers these thoughts on liminal space, a first cousin of thin places.

> Liminal space is an inner state and sometimes an outer situation where we can begin to think and act in new ways. It is where we are betwixt and between, having left one room or stage of life but not yet entered the next. We usually enter liminal space when our former way of being is challenged or changed—perhaps when we lose a job or a loved one, during illness, at the birth of a child, or a major relocation. It is a graced time, but often does not feel "graced" in any way. In such space, we are not certain or in control.
>
> The very vulnerability and openness of lim-

inal space allows room for something genuinely new to happen. We are empty and receptive—erased tablets waiting for new words. Liminal space is where we are most teachable, often because we are most humbled. Liminality keeps us in an ongoing state of shadow-boxing instead of ego-confirmation, struggling with the hidden side of things, and calling so-called normalcy into creative question.

Prayer

*Rejoice always, pray constantly,
give thanks in all circumstances;
for this is the will of God
in Christ Jesus for you.*

—1 Thessalonians 5:16–18 (RSV)

Prayer is a dialogue with God. In prayer, we can offer our praise, thanksgiving, and supplication. This simple practice begins a lifelong conversation with God that is an intimate part of our relationship with the Almighty. We can bring Him our joy, our hopes, and our desires. We can present our questions, our disappointments, and our tears. Thoughtful and deliberate, we must also listen for His response. We listen when we are quiet and know that He is there. Opportunity for our dialogue is continuous as we find endless ways throughout the day to reach out to God, who is always with us. As we read in the Bible, we are to "pray without ceasing," and when we do, we employ a powerful tool as we turn, turn, turn toward the Beloved.

The Psalm of David teaches us that even to offer a lament to God is a form of prayer. From the Book of Psalms, also known as the *prayer book* of the Bible, we find a model for how we are invited to bring all our feelings and concerns to God, not just our joyful expressions of gratitude and praise. We learn we do not have to pretend in our prayer, but that honest words of pain, frustration, and weariness have a valid place in this supernal conversation. Coming from the posture of loss and grief, we can lean into our sorrow and ask for deliverance. Our God knows us fully and loves us completely, and our openness in prayer at this time leads to a greater intimacy with our Savior.

Scripture

In the beginning
was the Word,
and the Word was with God,
and the Word was God.

—John 1:1 (RSV)

So many sacred words have nourished my aching soul. It always comes back to Scripture, always the Word. When I need to bolster myself up against fear or search for a hopeful word of encouragement, I always find it in the Bible. I keep a notebook on my desk and faithfully enter my favorite verses, the ones that called me to attention, as I happen upon them in my daily readings in my time of enlightenment. Powerful phrases created from inspiring ancient words are at my fingertips to shore me up as I seek a *good grief* and arrival at the other side of today. Daily I integrate them into my mind and soul referring to them often and counting on their truth to lift me up.

> Rejoice in your hope, be patient in tribulation, be constant in prayer. (Romans 12:12 RSV)

The Higher Self

> *A sense of freedom comes from the ability to live in the higher self no matter what is happening in your life.*

—Dr. Susan Jeffers, PhD

Most of us, most of the time, have circumstances in our lives that challenge us to stay in a higher spiritual place and not give in to our default tendencies of self-pity, anger, and resentment. To be in and stay in your higher self is a concept that resists explanation. It is such a powerful concept that a single definition seems almost arrogant.

The concept involves the true self and the separate self. The true self is the higher self, a divine spark deep within each of us that will never die. It has also been called a light, or a flame, one that is eternal and cannot be extinguished. The separate self is of this world and will die, in fact *must* die, as the higher self claims us in the end. Or should I say claims us in the beginning, for when the higher self reigns victorious, it heralds the beginning of our eternal life.

Hear your higher self calling you now louder than ever before. We are lifted up to this higher place where the view is better, allowing us to see more distinctly. In this profound place of light and love, we discover it will be a deliberate decision and effort to be the best person we can be as we endure this bereavement.

The Light Within

Again Jesus spoke to
them saying, "I am the
light of the world; he
who follows me will not
walk in darkness, but will
have the light of life.

—John 8:12 (RSV)

The higher self, or the true self, is often
compared to a light within us and often
called the *Light*. It strikes me that just as there
are multiple names for God (Wonderful
Counselor, Prince of Peace, Creator, Savior,
Alpha and Omega, Everlasting Lord, Yahweh,
and many more), there are multiple words to
describe this true self in each of us (higher
self, flame, spark, soul, the light, divine,
inner being). Perhaps it is because one name
falls short and is too small for the majesty of
which we speak. The concept is too deep and
wide and boundless to be captured in a single
word, or a few words. Perhaps there are no
words that are worthy of a thought so divine.

It is where we are with God and where God is with us. Emmanuel.

Our wounds, our losses, can let the light in. Light to shine on what we mourn. Light to provide a beacon of hope. Light to illuminate the path forward. Light to warm our chilly hearts. Light that enters us to heal. The Light can help us see a truth about our pain and sorrow, our wounds. Any loss, any hurt, any pain that we experience in our human state is an earthly loss. It is not an eternal loss. Even losing something as precious to us as a loved one represents an earthly loss. It is their ephemeral shell that is gone from us, but their soul lives on. Their absence is agonizing, and the separation is what hurts, but we know their spirit—their higher self ascends to be in communion with the Almighty, receiving the gift of eternal life.

As we walk in the darkness, through the darkness, and past the darkness of our pain and loss, be assured that the light will prevail. Isaiah 9:2 (RSV) offers this promise: "The people who walked in darkness have seen a great light; those who dwelt in a land of deep darkness, on them has light shined."

The Present Moment

*This is the day which
the Lord has made!
Let us rejoice and
be glad in it.*

—Psalm 118:24 (RSV)

We have always known to cherish each day, but never has this been more important than now. No matter what has been thrown in our path, today is a precious day of our life. Even a dark day has its gifts. Marianne Williamson says, "We do not heal the past by dwelling there. We heal the past by living fully in the present." Living fully in this, our now.

A sacrament in the Catholic church and many Christian churches is defined as a ritual that may impart *divine* grace. It is a term most often used in reference to baptism, the Eucharist, penance, and the anointing of the sick among others. But the phrase "sacrament of the present moment" was coined by a Jesuit priest who centuries ago penned the content, which would become a book of the same name. He used the term to elevate his belief that every *present moment* of our lives is an opportunity to receive the unmerited favor of *divine* grace. A sacrament was held as a blessed part of the faith, one of great value and importance to the church. Thus, to deem each ordinary moment something as holy as a sacrament demonstrated his deep conviction, that we are being spoken to by God at every moment of every day.

Acceptance and Letting Go

Acknowledge loss.
Acknowledge sorrow.
Acknowledge abandonment
and let it go.

The first step to healing is to accept that something happened and the blunt reality that it cannot be changed. There are no redos, and we cannot wish it away. Acceptance is not approval. Just because we accept something does not imply we are okay with it having happened. It is merely an acknowledgment of the occurrence, which smarts, when we would rather reject the shocking reality altogether. This is hard, because it requires a rational response instead of an emotional one. And at the beginning of our sojourn, we are suffocating and stumbling under the weight of our unrelenting emotions, making any rational response a challenge at best.

The second part is letting go. The two seem related yet somehow each is subtly unique. Acceptance feels like the heart is opening, allowing something in, and breathlessly holding on to it. But letting go is different. When we are ready, when we can release it, we let it go, and let it leave our heart. It is the letting go that frees us to open the door and see the path forward.

Making peace with the notion that our loss is not some random tragedy targeted at us personally is another crucial step in healing. Instead, we begin to realize that this is what happens, has happened, and will continue to happen to all of humanity since the dawn of civilization. Take a deep breath and one last time reaffirm that this dreadful thing occurred. No, it is not fair, it does not make sense, and things were not *supposed* to be this way. The glaring injustice of it is so disorienting that we lose our balance. And yet here it remains, the undeniable darkening ink blot on the white page of our lives. Another deep breath, then release it, and just let it go.

Let it all go…

Let Go of what is gone,
Be grateful for what remains,
Look forward to what is on the way.
(Author unknown)

An elusive ambiguity surrounds the concepts of acceptance and letting go. Thinking about acceptance feels like coming to terms with something that happened and cannot be changed. It is of the past. But part two, letting go, is pure liberation. Send it up in a balloon and kiss it goodbye! It is of the now. And the now is always more conducive to healing than the past.

Joy and Happiness

Choose Joy
Choose Happiness

Even in a time of loss, we can feel and experience joy. We may be quite unhappy about the way things have turned out, but even then, we have the opportunity to choose joy. If joy comes from within, we may always choose it; we gift ourselves. In the darkest of times, we can separate our thoughts from a negative place and invite them to a place of joy, a place where the beauty of life shines through.

Some believe joy is a deep personal state of mind, whereas happiness may be something more fleeting, born of external factors. Yet we want them both! Simply put, could it be that joy is from within and happiness is from without? Can we even differentiate between the two? Perhaps it is futile to try. The fact is both joy and happiness are strong positive emotions that can improve our mental state, boost our immune systems, and fortify our coping mechanisms. More importantly perhaps is that both joy and happiness can be chosen by each of us. We can always smile, look around, and count the blessings of today.

The Gift of Each Other

In the end,
what we really need more of
is each other.

—Anonymous

In the 1977 hit movie *Oh God* directed by Carl Reiner, George Burns stars as God appearing to John Denver's character Jerry Landers, who is the assistant manager of a grocery store. God asks Jerry to spread His Word to the rest of the world. Jerry is at first reluctant. He tries, but no one believes that God has really sent him, not even his wife. Later he and God talk, and Jerry asks if God controls our lives.

God explains that He gave us the world, and that it's up to us.

Jerry pleads with God and asks Him what they are supposed to do if they need help.

God answers, "That's why I gave you each other."

In the Sermon on the Mount, Jesus teaches the *beatitudes*, including this one that promises, "Blessed are they who mourn, for they shall be comforted." Interpretations of these tender words vary, and I am no theologian, but to me in their most simple form, they speak volumes. The meaning I derive from it is mostly face value, claiming that we who mourn will find comfort. That is enough for me—that is more than enough. The word *comfort* is derived from the Latin *comfortare*. "Com" means together and "fort" means strong or to strengthen greatly. We learn that "comfort" means much more than chicken noodle soup or fuzzy slippers. When we offer comfort, we offer a coming together with strength. It is two or more of us together, creating a certain strength we could not achieve alone. Together, or "com," we are strong, or "fort." We are strong together! Together with acts of kindness, generosity, sympathy, empathy, and most of all love, we reach out to give or receive this gift in time of need. Just like the words translate from one language to another, the acts of kindness also translate into support, consolation, relief from suffering and worry. A card, a flower, or some soup left at the door are all simple but not so small gestures reflecting how we come together to be strong. Spiritual gifts such as the promise of comfort, the promise of strength, and the promise of together let us know we are truly blessed.

We need each other, and we have each other. When someone needs help, we are there for them. When we need help, we can count on our brothers and sisters to be there for us. This is the Body of Christ, a blessed communion with our siblings in Christ. As the doctor and minister said to Michael in his final days, "Remember, we are related. We have the same Father."

"I wish I could have done more for you," one neighbor said to me apologetically.

But I assured her, "I always knew you were there and that I could call on you. That was a perfect gift, and that was gift enough."

Whether you are prone to resisting help (as I am) or one who receives it willingly, we have the assurance that help is abundantly available. I routinely declined the kind offers of others, but I was nonetheless comforted to receive them. Sometimes that is enough.

Perhaps we resist accepting help because it is so deeply personal. Can we allow someone else to know our deep wound or even touch it? That intimacy may be the highest form of the gift of each other. Until we are able to let someone close to our wound, we hold ourselves in a warm hug and rock gently side to side. With time, we will grow stronger, unwrap our arms, and open them wide to embrace others and to receive their embrace.

Order, Disorder, Reorder

Let us run with perseverance
The race that is set before us.

—Hebrews 12:1 (RSV)

Richard Rohr has written a great deal on the teaching of *order, disorder,* and *reorder.*

He explains, "It seems quite clear that we grow by passing beyond some perfect Order, through an often painful and seemingly unnecessary Disorder, to an enlightened Reorder or

317

resurrection. This is the universal pattern that connects and solidifies our relationships with everything around us. To grow toward love, union, salvation, or enlightenment, we must be moved from Order to Disorder and then ultimately to Reorder."

These are hard words to hear and harder yet to fully comprehend. We want *order* in our lives, and we long to be in charge. Order is our goal, as we try to minimize any *disorder* that may threaten the peaceful calm we have worked so hard to create. We like things the way they are in our predictable, safe little world. Then along comes *disorder* to undo all we have accomplished, leaving us threatened and confused. Sadly, we can object all we want, but life unfolds unexpectedly and sometimes painfully jerks us out of our cozy, orderly lives. We are thrust into a whirlwind of *disorder* against our will. We can barely understand it, much less navigate the terrain with any certainty. It hurts here, and we want to go back. But this is a one-way street. We are forced to either stay in *disorder* or move on to *reorder*, an unknown place, fraught with frightening uncertainty.

Our life before our loss was a place of *order*. We did not even appreciate that *order*, until it was taken away from us. We so foolishly thought we could protect it indefinitely. In this place, we come face-to-face with grief. We do not like it here in the depths of *disorder*, and we want out. But we must stay here as we process and heal, and when we are ready, we move forward. Reorder awaits, and we acknowledge that we are changed. This new phase represents our growth and our advancement toward a higher understanding. Suddenly, the light shines in as we welcome a reassuring peace and a new way of thinking. I can almost see the bluebirds and the snowflakes in the distance. A new life, a changed life, a richer life is ours if we can be aware and allow this inevitable transition to take place.

Fake It Till You Make It

Now faith is the assurance of things hoped for, the conviction of things not seen.

—Hebrews 11:1 (RSV)

Shortly after Michael died, I heard from one of his colleagues in psychiatry. They had worked together years ago, remained friends, and she and her husband came to our wedding. A dear soul, she had even visited us in the hospital. She quickly contacted me in case I wanted to talk. Since she knew Michael and our situation so well, it sounded like a good idea. I had already started to grapple with my almost immediate repulsion at the thought of having to endure another grief. It was early December, so only weeks after the painful departure, and my feelings were raw. I could hardly speak for the crying, but Annie patiently guided me through the session. It was all so fresh that I struggled to put my thoughts into intelligible words, but she heard me loud and clear. I declared, "I am not going through this again. I just cannot bear it!" She reassured me I could choose my own path, and it did not have to be as before.

As we wrapped things up, she said to me with strong assertiveness, "Here is my advice to you: fake it till you make it!" I asked her what she meant, and she explained I needed to try to imitate what I wished to be true for me, and that if I keep telling myself that is how I feel, the brain will eventually believe it. I could tell myself to practice smiling, then smiling will gradually become easier. I could tell myself this was not going to be as bad this time and really mean it because that is what I wished and what I intended; my positive attitude would help make it happen. I could focus on inspirational words and thoughts and internalize them until they became truth for me. I could tell myself I am going to survive and get through this in a healthy manner, and I would keep saying it until it was true. I could keep feeding myself uplifting messages of healing even if I did not fully feel it yet, and my mind would start to believe it, and my heart would be close behind.

Those two rascals, self-pity and bitterness, may well show up and try to crash the party. Even when we are trying to "fake it," these emotions can creep in. If they appear, go as quickly as possible to a place and find something from which there stems bountiful gratitude and happiness. Step outside and breathe in some fresh air and sunshine, gaze at a favorite photo, savor a cookie. Put a big bowl of shiny red apples in the middle of the kitchen table and delight in the simple glory. Let some cheerful music brighten the day, and remember that laughter is the best medicine. Smile intentionally, appreciating what a powerful mood changer it can be. Grab on to the promise of reaching past what we cannot control to the place where we do have a choice, and it will pull us through the moment.

This brawny advice was a strong tool. I was familiar with the phrase "Fake it till you make it," but in this context, it was truly empowering. Already a believer of the mind-body connection, I did not have to be convinced of its validity. Annie's wise words fell onto my willing spirit, fortifying my determination to heal in a healthier way.

The Power of Suggestion and Positive Thinking

I think I can,
I think I can,
I think I can.

—The Little Engine
that Could

The power of suggestion can be friend or foe on the quest for *good grief*. The suggestion that this normal part of life is going to be hard and hurt and take a long time can strongly influence our actions and reactions negatively. Similarly, the suggestion that our choices for how to cope have a major role to play in our healing can be just as powerful on the plus side. The sister of the power of suggestion is the power of positive thinking, slightly different but another significant tool with its own persuasive capacity.

Importantly, we must also be aware that there is a power of negative thinking and what it can do to us. The power of suggestion is from external sources, but the power of positive or negative thinking is from within us. Ask yourself if deep emotions or sorrows are external or internal, and take responsibility for your role in how you respond. Stay aware of your thoughts and the power they hold. If you *think you can*, that is half the battle.

Intentional Breathing

Then the Lord God formed
man of dust from the ground,
and breathed into his
nostrils the breath of life;
and the man became
a living being.

—Genesis 2:7 (RSV)

Breath represents life itself. It is the very essence of our temporal existence. From the first breath we take as we come crying out of our mother's womb, till our last breath when we leave this earth, it is breathing that defines our mortal status. When that precious gift of breath is gone, our earthly shell falls away. When we are out of breath, or short of breath, we stop and give that our full attention. If we cannot breathe, nothing else matters.

Some say breath is the presence of the Holy Spirit within us. The word *Spirit* comes from the Latin for "breath." When first we inhale this earthly air, it seems to fill us with the spirit of the *divine*. It is God within us, Emmanuel, in the most profound way. It is this entity we call air, which we cannot see or touch, that we draw into our lungs. Air changes to breath, with a life-giving force that is nothing short of miraculous. Similarly, we cannot see or touch God, but if we draw Him in, as we draw in breath, we receive His life-giving energy. It sustains us through every day and night as our silent companion providing strength and well-being. Surely our breath is bound closely to our higher self, our flame, our light, reaffirming that God is truly within us.

There is genuine healing in breathing—intentional breathing. Meditation and contemplation practices begin with centering on breathing. By doing so, we can purposefully embrace and commune with the spirit of life within us, that is borne in every precious breath we inhale and exhale. Through our breath, which is life, we can enter that place deep within us where the Almighty dwells. Our physical, mental, and emotional healing can be strengthened by this treasured ancient practice.

The Garden

I think of Heaven
as a Garden
Where I shall find again
Those dear ones
Who have made my world.

—Minnie Aumônier

Descriptions of the Garden of Eden elevate the setting to *paradise*, likening it to that promised us for eternal life. Our earthly gardens can be a place for healing and inspiration and a reminder that a greater paradise awaits. Throughout my years of bereavement, my garden has sustained me. A handful of ashes from both husbands are buried there, watered in with my tears. But those tears were transformed into the abundant delight and exuberance that greets me there now, on my journey toward a *good grief.*

If we enter a garden with open eyes and an open heart, we discover treasures to lift our spirits and distract us from sadness. Deep down we know that here we are connecting with nature and God and tapping into something majestic. It is almost as if we are being allowed a tiny glimpse into the hereafter, especially *après la pluie*. The rain ends and sunshine floods in with dazzling light. Not a cloud in the sky, and the freshness of the air defies description. The earth is cool and sparkles as glistening raindrops cling to a leaf or rose petal. In our own brokenness, let us remember that the rain in our hearts will stop—it always does. And "good times" will follow. The sun will appear again to brighten the day and dry both the raindrops and our tears.

In our backyard gardens and in the gardens of our life, we lose one treasure and gain another. We embrace each phase of life and growth as it surges, then fades, and appreciate the majesty of it all the more. Instead of dwelling on what is lost, we look to the new creation, a stunning manifestation of the eternal lesson. Season after season we witness our "bit of earth" awakening to growth and blooming then fading into dormancy or death. Thus, the garden becomes the ultimate teacher of death and rebirth—loss and renewal. Where rebirth and renewal come together, we find the true meaning of hope.

The Gift

My earliest days in grief seminary after Michael's death made me wonder if meaning and purpose in my life had survived or if I had lost that too. I desperately searched for answers and strength. Daily meditations and online devotionals became the cream in my coffee. A few grief books I had not previously read presented a fresh perspective. Through it all, Scripture was my anchor. Some messages resounded with more personal impact than others, and I was intent on retaining them. These words made me feel better; these words offered encouragement and hope. These were the words that spoke to my soul.

As I examined the newfound gems in my spiritual treasure chest, I observed there were four messages that kept appearing. Repeatedly, I noticed a key phrase or a variation of one. I chose a letter to represent each gem, then happily discovered they fit seamlessly into a blessed mnemonic. I received my GIFT!

G—Gratitude always

No matter where we are in our lives or how disrupted things might be, we are called to acknowledge that we have blessings for which to be grateful.

I—I am with you

He is always with us. This is truly one of our Lord's most intimate promises. We can rely on this assurance and discover that we are never truly alone. It is the great gift of comfort from the Great Comforter.

F—Fear not

"Be not afraid." Some claim that this message is stated 365 times in the Bible. There are just as many critics who say otherwise. Either way, the suggestion of remembering this empowering concept on a daily basis has great merit.

T—Trust Me

The virtue of trust is a belief in the reliability, strength, and truth of God as we live each day. It calls us to surrender to Him and have confidence in His word. With an open heart, we long for the grace of trusting God in all things.

G—Gratitude always
I—I am with you
F—Fear not
T—Trust Me

After graduating from grief seminary, I held close to the truths I had learned. Many of the lessons were familiar to me, but I wanted to process them till they became second nature. As these treasured concepts and practices were integrated into my mind and soul, I found direction, strength, and hope. And I will always treasure my GIFT, as I share it with you now.

11

A Farewell to Fear

When I was ready
I went back to the lunch counter
in the True Story Café.
I realized I was still hungry.
I looked at the menu and ordered Today's Special,
A Survivor Sundae.
It was a double scoop of Gratitude
Nestled between Scoops of
Resilience, Fortitude, and Hope.
Smothered with Whipped creamy love,
it was topped with a joyful cherry
and surrounded with sprinkles of
Bluebirds and Snowflakes.
It richly fed my soul!

*A*gain, I ask: What *is* the true story? After years under the influence of the *dark side of grief*, I am now more able to see the truth, to see the light. The eyes of my heart and soul are wide open and free of the tears that obstructed my view for so long. The truth is in every scoop of gratitude and every joyful cherry. The truth is in every breath we take and in every sacred wound. It is there in prayer, acceptance, and letting go. It lives in your higher self. The truth is what held my hand and guided me as I found my way to a *good grief*.

There is a certain emotional resilience that is the inevitable result of enduring, then surviving a crisis or great loss. All the studies or inner preparations in the world are no substitute for the actual atoning by fire. As we emerge from the ashes, we discover that a certain refinement has occurred. We now know there is no answer to *why*, and we quit asking. Life seems shorter and shorter, but even in our sorrow, we have joy in this present and real day of our life. No matter what has been lost, we can look around and be grateful for what remains. A closer sense of our Creator permeates each precious day, surer than ever that He is with us always.

It starts with a goldfish. Next, a hamster or a parakeet. Loss and the ensuing grief often start at a tolerable level in childhood. The child is assured that the missing pet is happily in heaven and told this is part of life. The episode passes, and without fully understanding, on some level the child does understand. It is the blessing of juvenile acceptance and a lesson well learned. How I wish we could hold on to that childlike faith as our losses get more difficult.

Perhaps as we have matured, we have grown too far away from God to hear the quiet consolation. Like the parents in *The Polar Express*, who do not hear the magical jingle bell left under the Christmas tree. The children hear it and wonder why their parents cannot. Then there is the story of the three-year-old girl who asks her parents if she can speak to her newborn baby brother in private. Her parents agree but listen in on the baby monitor. The sister closes the door and approaches her brother's cradle. After a moment of silence, they heard her say, "Baby, please tell me what heaven is like. I am starting to forget." Charles Dickens put it this way, "It is no small thing, when they, who are so fresh from God, love us."

We can create our own blessing of acceptance if we learn our lesson well. We may have lost that intimate childhood connection to the *divine*, but as we seek God and His will for us, we will find it once again. Henri Nouwen has provided comforting words and thoughts to me for years through his daily meditations. A former Dutch Catholic priest, well-known author and theologian, he offers this insightful reflection,

> Jesus invites us to look at the reality of our existence and reveals this harsh reality as the way to a new life. The core message of Jesus is that real joy and peace can never be reached while bypassing suffering and death, but only by going right through them. We could say: "We really have no choice." Indeed, who

escapes suffering and death?
Yet there is still a choice. We
can deny the reality of life or
we can face it. When we face
it not in despair, but with
the eyes of Jesus, we discover
that where we least expect
it, something is hidden that
holds a promise stronger than
death itself. Jesus lived his life
with a trust that God's love
is stronger than death and
that death, therefore does
not have the last word. He
invites us to face the painful
reality of our existence with
the same trust.

With an ambiguous illusion, there is one
image, but it can be interpreted in two different ways. The well-known sketch of the "Wife
and the Mother-in-Law" provides an illustrative
example. One person may see the young wife
looking away to the right over her shoulder.
Another would see the older woman in profile
with her head nodding down. Both images exist,

but our brain may only allow one to come into view. In grief and loss, we may be confronted with a similar ambiguous illusion. There exists a representation of our broken world, but one person will see it one way, and someone else will have a different view. Neither is right or wrong, instead it demonstrates the extent of our singularity in both self and situation. Often with these illusions, both images become clear after some extended observation. The revelation feels abrupt when the second image suddenly comes into view. Similarly, we may have processed our loss in one way for a while, then later with a jolt become aware that we are seeing it differently. We are finally able to visualize the whole of what has shaken our world, rather than just a part.

Strengthened by our newfound emotional resilience, childlike acceptance, and the ability to discern any ambiguous illusion, a deeper awareness can emerge. When we are ready, knee-jerk reactions and blinding emotions recede. It is then we can experience a more authentic consciousness. It is our waking up, our being fully alive in each day, our being one with the *sacrament of the present moment.*

Somewhere between the vastness of yesterday and each elusive tomorrow, we find ourselves wobbling on the tightrope of today. How we struggle to keep our balance! We glance down for a safety net below and discover our brothers and sisters waiting with open arms to catch us if we fall. And we recognize the Almighty within them who calls our name. Each careful step forward brings us closer to a new beginning. And each lesson learned along the way strengthens us to move ahead, as we keep our eyes peeled to the future, and never look back.

Richard Rohr has many teachings on the *sacred wound*. He says,

> When we can trust the transformative pattern, and that God is in the suffering, our wounds become sacred wounds. The actual and ordinary life journey becomes itself the godly journey. We trust God to be in all things, even in sin and suffering.

Because we do not fully understand the complexity of suffering, we may call it a mystery. We cannot tame it because it is so infused with uncertainties. Our humanness is exposed as we recognize the *divine* so near. Father Richard tells us our pain can bring us to a deeper understanding, a path to salvation. Our wound is sacred in the possibilities it offers for our redemption and growth. It is sacred in the way it sustains us through the pain, to the other side, giving us hope. It is sacred in the way it repeats the eternal promise of resurrection. As Jesus said,

> Truly, truly, I say to you,
> unless a grain of wheat falls
> into the earth and dies,
> it remains alone;
> but if it dies, it bears
> much fruit.
> (John 12:24 RSV)

My *sacred wounds* have allowed my soul to see what was once hidden. Saint-Exupery tells us in the classic *Le Petit Prince*, "What is essential is invisible to the eye." Through the suffering, a veil was lifted, a thin veil in a thin place between perception and reality. I see now I am not alone in my suffering, and many of my brethren share my plight. It is only through my wound that I learn a great truth and now may share it with others. The truth is that my loss was something of an earthly matter. My smaller false self is deeply hurt, but my higher true self can be ever stronger and see more clearly. That which is of the eternal world cannot be lost because God has promised He will always be with us and our true destination is to be with Him. My earthly false self has been destroyed by this loss, until through quiet contemplation and awareness, my higher self emerged to protect and guide me. It is this spark of the *divine* that lives in all of us. A new relationship with loss can evolve as appreciation of its blessings are revealed.

Ultimately, we seek a oneness with God. The divine infinite being, the I Am, hails the tiny spark of our higher self, and the two are summoned together. God suffers with us in our loss, in our time of pain, and promises to be there with us. At the Last Supper, He broke the bread, reminding us of our own brokenness, and that our brokenness is a path, a part of our life. In our time of loss, we become keenly aware of our human existence and our mortality. We know that earth shall pass away, but God and His promises will not pass away. When we hang our star on that eternal prize, knowing all the rest is fleeting, we can walk out into this world and know nothing can really ever hurt us again.

O God, our help
in ages past,
Our hope for years to come.
Our shelter from
the stormy blast.
And our eternal home.
(Isaac Watts, 1719)

On the morning of Michael's memorial service, I awoke and read this Henri Nouwen daily meditation, waiting for me in my e-mail. It felt so personal and so intended for me, to help me through this impossible day, this impossible time in my life. And it did. Entitled "Passages to New Life."

It seems we are always passing from one phase to the next, gaining and losing someone, someplace, something. You live all these passages in an environment where you are constantly tempted to be destroyed by resentment, by anger, and by a feeling of being put down. The losses remind you constantly that all isn't perfect and it doesn't always happen for you the way you expected; that perhaps you had hoped events would not have been so painful, but they were; or that you expected something from certain relationships that never materialized. You find yourself disillusioned with the irrevocable personal losses: your health, your lover, your job, your hope, your dream. Your whole life is filled with losses, endless losses. And every time there are losses there are choices to be made. You choose to live your losses as passages to anger, blame, hatred, depression, and resentment, or you choose to let these losses be passages to something new, something wider, and deeper. The question is not how to avoid loss and make it not happen, but how to choose it as a passage, as an exodus to greater life and freedom.

No, we cannot avoid loss, but we can and must respect it. There is no yardstick long enough, no ruler wide enough, to measure the scope of any loss, pain, or grief. Unique to each person, it defies quantification. Whatever hardship a person is dealt, at that time, there is nothing more difficult in the world for them to endure. The loss of a job or close relationship can be devastating. A serious, terrifying diagnosis or destructive divorce can be paralyzing. The pain is real, and indescribable. If a mother loses her baby at birth, does she mourn it briefly because she held it in her arms fewer times than the three-year-old at home? Perhaps she mourns it even more. My marriages with Mike and Michael were vastly different as calculated by time, but does this mean I mourn Michael any less because of brevity?

> *It is best if we make*
> *no assumptions about*
> *someone else's loss.*
> *It is too personal,*
> *too inestimable.*
> *And it does not matter.*
> *Yours is yours, and*
> *mine is mine.*

My respect for loss was further fortified by a conversation remembered from six years ago. I recall the morning when my daughters and I sat in the hospital waiting room with Pastor Anna as Mike had a procedure done.

I had asked Anna how she could keep up the emotional task of pastoral care for families facing medical or life emergencies. I imagined it took a heavy toll on her generous heart. But she surprised us with her quick response, "It's so rich." She started to elaborate, and I remember my initial confusion at her comment. Six years ago, I could not begin to fully comprehend what she meant, but now it seems there really were no words big enough for that little speck of divine truth. Now a few years older and tempered with my subsequent loss, I finally understand. For all the sadness and emotion in end-of-life events, there is a corresponding richness to be had. These are sacred moments for both the soul on the threshold of eternity and for those left behind. It is rich with wonder at this great mystery of life. It is rich with the fullness of support as others lift us up and carry us home. It is rich with gratitude for that person in our lives. It is rich with love and truth. *It is so, so rich.*

Sister Joan Chittister is featured here in a daily meditation from Richard Rohr and the CAC. The wisdom in her powerful words resonated within me to my deepest core as

I ingested the following piece entitled "Life Goes On,"

The sense of being stranded in the midst of life… is enough to drain a person's very personality until there is little left to recognize. Where did the joy go all of a sudden? Where did the feeling of self-confidence disappear to in the midst of this emptiness? Just yesterday life was clear and vibrant. Today it is endlessly bleak. The darkness is unyielding. Nothing helps; nothing takes it away.

There is no light here, we think. But we think wrong.

There is a light in us that only darkness itself can illuminate. It is the glowing calm that comes over us when we finally surrender to the ultimate truth of creation: that there is a God and we are not it... Then the clarity of it all is startling. Life is not about us; we are about the project of finding Life. At that moment, spiritual vision illuminates all the rest of life. And it is that light that shines in darkness.

Only the experience of our own darkness gives us the light we need to be of help to others whose journey into the dark spots of life is only just beginning. It's then that our own taste of darkness qualifies us to be an illuminating part of the human expedition. Without that, we are only words, only false witnesses to the truth of what it means to be pressed to the ground and rise again.

The light we gain in darkness is the awareness that, however bleak the place of darkness was for us, we did not die there. We know now that life begins again on the other side of the darkness. Another life. A new life. After the death, the loss, the rejection, the failure, life does go on. Differently, but on. Having been sunk into the cold night of...despair—and having survived it—we rise to new light, calm and clear and confident that what will be, will be enough for us.

I completely identified with these wise words and read them over and over. Yes, we were in a place of darkness, but we did not die there. Life begins on the other side, a new life. We were sunk into the cold night of despair, and we survived it! These words can be internalized into our very being, and with that joyous recognition, that will be enough.

The pressing question is how to survive this transition in a positive way. We remind ourselves that pain, disappointment, and the many faces of loss are predictable parts of life. We are learning that we have choices and are not totally at the mercy of our out-of-control feelings. When tired of crying, practice smiling! When self-pity shows up, take note and vow never to be a victim. To be a victim or *not* to be a victim is based on our self-perception, and now our view from the vantage point of the higher self is crystal clear.

Resolve to do the internal work, whatever that is for you. Recognize it as a valuable key, powerful enough to free you from this bondage. Resources and ways to deal with this most difficult time are abundantly available, and it is our decision to seek them out or not. The internal work is hard, but it is supposed to be hard. If it were not hard, the payoff would not be so satisfying. The *hard* is what makes it great. The *hard* is what pays your dues. The *hard* is what ransoms your tears. Respect it and trust that this is your way out, your truth, and an open path to a new tomorrow.

Glimpses of survival start to appear and take over raw landscapes once ravaged by fear and sorrow. Little by little, we begin to think about what is left of our life and what future may be in store. A frightening shift could be imminent, but deep down, we know fear is useless; what is needed is trust. We open ourselves to love, all possibilities of love, knowing love is the only currency. Brotherly love, familial love, romantic love, the love of animals and nature, the love of God—how they all enrich our lives.

Perhaps it is time to start something fresh and trust in the magic of new beginnings. Let the goodness in, let it all in! Be gentle with yourself and know that after a great loss, life will be forever changed, but life does go on. "In the divine womb of God, life is always born again" (Henri Nouwen).

I think back on my first visit to the True Story Café. I did not order that *grief sandwich*, and I never would have. In fact, I was still looking at the menu when it was served to me. Is that not the way life can be? And for all of us, there is just no way of telling what might come along on any given day, and there is not a thing we can do about it. It is life happening. "Today's Special" is forever changing. One day it will make you sick, and another day, it will feed your soul. Whichever it is, we are called to stay in our higher self as we accept what life brings, all the while absorbing the lessons laid before us. This is our true story.

I bid farewell to Darth Vader and the *dark side of grief*, I bid farewell to the *warden* and his *prison*, and I bid farewell to *fear*. You no longer have control over me—I have escaped! I escaped from an emotional nightmare where I was held against my will. I escaped from the subtle bondage of social mores that intimidated me. I escaped from a gripping fear, a fear of endless unknowns. My old world is gone and has been replaced by the truth of now. As I choose to grow, I learn a certain surrender can be simultaneously humbling and freeing. I will not squander the hour of my peace and healing, rich with the grace of God. Instead, I will celebrate it each day with joyful gratitude.

In this blessed
Sacrament of the
present moment,
I am a cloudless blue sky,
And the light in me
Calls to the light in you
With joyful anticipation
That we may provide
Gifts to one another
For a peaceful
journey home.

Amen.

For
Michael and Michael,
Beloved husbands,
Who gave me joy in life
And enlightenment
in death.

REFERENCES AND PERMISSIONS

Aumônier, Minnie. 1865–1952. Quote. Public domain.

Author unknown. "Bed Is Too Small," folk song.

Author unknown. "Star Light, Star Bright," according to poetryfoundation.org.

Barrie, J. M. 1904. *Peter Pan.* Public domain.

Bradstreet, Anne. 1612–1672. *To My Dear and Loving Husband.* Public domain.

Cash, Johnny. 1956. *I Walk the Line.* Sun Records.

Chittister, Joan D. 2015. Excerpts from *Between the Dark and the Daylight: Embracing the Contradictions of Life.* Used by permission of Image Books, an imprint of Random House, a division of Penguin Random House LLC. All rights reserved.

Davis, Katherine. 1939. "Let All Things Now Living." Now in public domain.

Denver, John. 1966. "Leaving on a Jet Plane." Warner Brother labels. Recorded by Peter, Paul, and Mary.

Dunham, Reverend Robert E. *Anglican Commendation*. Used with permission. Original text from the Funeral of Diana Princess of Wales from westminster-abby.com.

Gibran, Kahlil. 2014. *Sand and Foam*. Penguin Random House. Used with Permission.

Hamilton, Ruth Hulbert. 1958. Last verse from "Song for a Fifth Child." *Ladies Home Journal*. Used with permission from the family.

Jacobs, Mary. 1910. *The Pony Engine*. Kindergarten Review. Later version called *Little Engine that Could*. Public Domain.

Jones, George. 1979. *He Stopped Loving Her Today*. Epic Label.

Kübler-Ross, Elisabeth. 2005. *On Grief and Grieving*. Simon and Schuster.

Loggins, Dave. 1974. *Please Come to Boston*. Epic Label.

Lowell, Amy. 1919. *Decade*. Public domain.

Mitchell, Stephen. 1982. "The Tenth Elegy" from *Selected Poetry of Rainer Maria Rilke* by Rainer Maria Rilke, edited and translated by Stephen Mitchell. Used by permission of Random House an imprint and division of Penguin Random House LLC. All rights reserved.

Nouwen, Henri. 1994. *Show Me the Way*. Reprinted by arrangement with The Crossroad Publishing Company. www.crossroadpublishing.com.

———. 2004. *Finding My Way Home: Pathways to Life and the Spirit*. Reprinted by agreement with The Crossroad Publishing Company. www.crossroadpublishing.com.

———. 2006. *Here and Now*. Reprinted by arrangement with The Crossroad Publishing Company. www.crossroadpublishing.com.

Nouwen, Henri., Donald McNeill, and Douglas Morrison. 2006. *Compassion: A Reflection on the Christian Life*. Image Books, Doubleday, a division of Penguin Random House. Illustrator Joel Filartiga.

Prince, William Meade. 1950. *The Southern Part of Heaven*. University of North Carolina Press. Used with permission.

Richardson, Jan. *Blessing for the Brokenhearted* from *The Cure for Sorrow: A Book of Blessings for Times of Grief*. Orlando, Florida: Wanton Gospeller Press. Used by permission. janrichardson.com.

Rohr, Richard. 2004. *Adam's Return*. Reprinted by arrangement with The Crossroad Publishing Company. www.crossroadpublishing.com.

———. 2019. *The Universal Christ*. (Convergent Books, an imprint of Crown Publishing Group, a division of Penguin Random House LLC), NY. Book design by Andrea Lau. Jacket design by Sarah Horgan.

———. 2020. *The Wisdom Pattern: Order, Disorder, Reorder*. Franciscan Media. Used with permission. franciscanmedia.org.

Rossitti, Christina. 1872. "In the Bleak Midwinter." Public domain.

Rubin, Gretchen. Quote used with permission.

Saint-Exupery, Antoine de. 1943. *The Little Prince*. Reynal and Hitchcock.

Shakespeare, William. "If It Be Thus to Dream, Still Let Me Sleep." Public domain.

Susan Jeffers quote. Permission granted from Mark Shelmerdine, CEO, Susan Jeffers, LLC. susanjeffers.com.

Taylor, James. 1968. *Carolina in My Mind*. Apple Records.

Watts, Isaac. 1719. *O God Our Help in Ages Past*. Public domain.

Williamson, Marianne. 1996. *A Return to Love*. HarperPerennial, a division of HarperCollins Publishers. Used with permission.

About the Author

*B*orn and raised in the eastern United States, Gail Norwood spent her youth in Wooster, Ohio, and Williamsburg, Virginia, where she developed a fondness for charming small college towns and appreciation of life with four seasons. After graduating from Emory and Henry College with a degree in elementary education, she began a twenty-five-year career as a flight attendant with American Airlines. Gail and her husband, Mike, had two daughters and lived in Dallas, Texas, for many years until a convergence of circumstances brought them to a new life in Chapel Hill, North Carolina. There, amid the demands and joys of work and family life, they created and maintained their dream garden on two acres, which eventually became their shared passion and the subject of several magazine articles and numerous garden tours. Now, retired and blessed with four grandchildren, Gail remains grateful for family, dear friends, and time to watch her bluebirds.

www.gailnorwood.com
Fb.com/gailnorwoodauthor
Instagram.com/gailnorwoodauthor

CPSIA information can be obtained
at www.ICGtesting.com
Printed in the USA
BVHW081531130422
633717BV00001B/1

9 781638 146216